QUICK & EASY BANNER DESIGNS

Carol Jean Harms

CPH.
SAINT LOUIS

In memory of Emma Anna Polack
(nee Rippe Wellhausen)

The "banner lady" of Grace Lutheran Church,
Molalla, Oregon
January 5, 1906 – January 26, 1995

Thank you, Kendra

All Scripture quotations, unless otherwise indicated, are taken from the HOLY BIBLE, NEW INTERNA-TIONAL VERSION®. NIV®. Copyright © 1973, 1978, 1984 by International Bible Society. Used by permission of Zondervan Publishing House. All rights reserved.

Scripture quotations marked KJV are from the King James or Authorized Version of the Bible.

Copyright © 1996 Concordia Publishing House
3558 S. Jefferson Avenue, St. Louis, MO 63118-3968
Manufactured in the United States of America

Library of Congress Cataloging-in-Publication Data

Harms, Carol Jean, 1940–
    Quick and easy banner designs / Carol Jean Harms.
      p.   cm.
    ISBN 0-570-04842-7
    1. Church pennants. 2. Christian art and symbolism. I. Title.
BV168.F5H38 1996
246'.55—dc20   95-37809

3   4   5   6   7   8   9   10   03   02   01   00   99

Contents

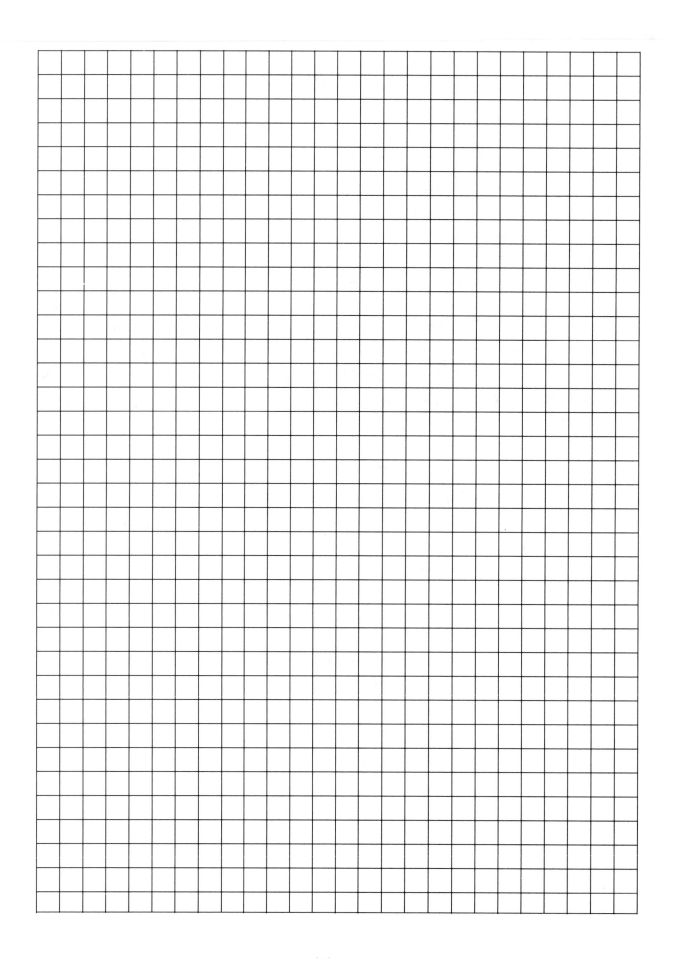

Preface

My first attempts at making banners were done at night after my five children were in bed. By 4 a.m. the banners were usually ready to be hung. No stores were open that late at night. Therefore, any mistakes made or difficulties encountered with fabrics became the creative seeds for my methods, directions, shortcuts, and solutions. I wanted a beautiful banner and yet I wanted to be able to go to bed before the sun came up!

More recently, on a whim, I decided that if I could find blue fabric in my basement, and if I could transfer a 3-by-5-inch banner design into a 36-by-60-inch banner in four hours exactly, I would use the banner that evening for a city-wide Lutheran Women's Missionary League prayer service at Beautiful Savior Lutheran Church in Winnipeg. Otherwise, I would complete the banner the next day to be used for other occasions. *I used every shortcut I knew and invented three more* in order to complete my "four-hour wonder" with one minute to spare! "Quick and easy" *is* possible!

The most important pieces of advice I can give you from my experience with "midnight specials" and an ongoing need for quick and easy banners can be summed up in the "Big 8" printed below.

CAROL JEAN'S BIG 8

1. Select background fabric that does *not* need lining, hemming, or a dowel at the bottom. If the desired color is not available in such a fabric, more time and effort will be needed.

2. Select fabrics for the design pieces, letters, and ribbons that can be *glued* rather than fused.

3. Gluing is the *quickest and least expensive* method for assembling banners. Preshrinking and fusing are eliminated. *NOTE: Do not use materials that will not bond with glue.*

4. Avoid problems by making trial samples with scraps from any materials that have not been used previously on banners.

5. Practice new techniques on scraps first. Once mastered, use the technique for assembling the banner.

6. Have extra "fusibles" on hand for emergencies—fusible interfacing, fusible web, paper-backed fusible web, fusible thread, and a roll of ¼-inch fusible web. These materials come to the rescue when glue will not bond fabrics that are of unknown fiber content or certain 100% polyesters.

7. Make transparencies of all the banner designs at one time. Enlarge the alphabet patterns 200% on the copy machine for instant tracing. The symbols, designs, and wording may be interchanged or used to create a custom-made banner of any size for any occasion.

8. Keep a notebook of what works and what does not; then buy accordingly for making future banners. Record brand names of the fusible materials and keep samples of the fabrics.

PART 1

A Quick and Easy Reference Guide

THE 17 BASIC STEPS OF ASSEMBLY

Step 1

Select the design for the banner and make a *transparency* of it.

Step 2

Trace the banner pattern:

2.1 Use an *overhead projector* for tracing the design with soft lead *pencil* onto the dull side of *white freezer wrap paper* cut to the exact size of the finished banner.

2.2 Do not trace each letter. Instead draw a *rectangle* around each word.

2.3 Trace the letters with a pencil on a separate sheet of freezer wrap paper for cutting. Trace only one pattern for each letter (e.g., trace one *N* even though there are seven identical *Ns* in the wording).

2.4 The exception to 2.3 is if the letters have delicate parts or thin lines that would stretch out of shape or fray; then trace a pattern for *each* of those letters.

Step 3

Prepare the shopping list for the banner:

3.1 Record the exact finished length and width of the banner. Add on 3 inches for the dowel insert at the top and 2 inches for the bottom hem. Allow 1 inch for each side hem. Side and bottom hems may be optional depending upon the type of fabric selected.

3.2 Determine the amount of *fusible inter-facing* needed for lining the banner if the fabric warrants it. Allow at least 12 inches extra for test samples.

3.3 Measure the amount of *fabric* needed for all of the design pieces of the same color. *NOTE: If the fabric has a nap, the pieces may need to be laid out in the same up-and-down direction and will require more yardage. Allow extra fabric if it is to be preshrunk.*

3.4 Measure the length of any *ribbon or fringe* to be used. Allow at least 1 inch extra for each corner and another 12 inches for test samples.

3.5 Purchase approximately ½ yard soft *black felt* for outlining the design unless white felt is required.

3.6 Determine the amount of *paper-backed fusible web* needed for attaching the banner pieces to the background if using Step 15.

3.7 White freezer wrap paper is necessary for Steps 8–14 for gluing the pieces to the banner.

3.8 Record the length and width of *dowel(s)* needed (refer to Steps 17.1 and 17.5) and length of *cord or chain* for holding the rod. Purchase *nails or eye screws* for the end part of the dowel.

3.9 Check that all other supplies are on hand. These supplies are found at fabric stores:
  • cardboard cutting board with grid
  • cutting wheel with vinyl cutting pad
  • plastic square (L-shaped ruler)
  • pins with ball heads
  • sharp scissors

- thick, tacky craft glue
- blue and white tailor's chalk
- tracing wheel
- tracing paper suitable for fabric
- Flexcurv brand tracing tool
- magnetic pin holder
- black permanent marker (see Step 8.1)
- sequins—variety of colors in 5 and 10 mm size

The following supplies may be found in a hardware department or store:
- 2 metal yardsticks
- 2 48-inch yardsticks
- carpenter's square

A homemade 24-by-24-inch wool-covered plywood board is helpful for fusing fabrics.

Post-It brand glue stick (or another pressure-sensitive adhesive such as Aleene's Tack-It Over & Over brand) and double-stick tape are office supply items.

3.10 Include for the shopping trip a ziplock bag containing black rug yarn or ¼-inch wide black felt strips cut into 24-inch segments; 3-inch letters cut from black, white, and other colors of fabric; your shopping list; and this book, which contains the design and color scheme.

Step 4

Select fabrics according to their colors:

4.1 At the store, arrange the fabrics that are suitable for banners next to each other as the colors would be on the banner background. Match the color number on the design with the color key on the back cover of this book and read page 28 for more information on number and color codes.

4.2 Place strips of felt or yarn (from the ziplock bag) between the colors of the selected fabric.

4.3 Stand as far away as possible to see how well the colors harmonize. Keep changing fabrics until the most ideal combination is reached. Try to use only those fabrics that can be glued.

4.4 Place various-colored letters on the background fabric. Check to see which letter's color is most visible and yet blends with the color scheme of the banner. This most likely will be the color to use for the lettering. If in doubt, use white letters on a dark background and black letters on a light background.

4.5 Hold any trim, ribbon, or fringes on the arrangement of fabrics to see what looks the best. Be sure gold trim is highly reflective, even from a distance. Gold trim for the design line (such as for a cross) may vary in width from ⅛ to 1 inch depending on what is available. Select the width that best fits the integrity of the design. Refer to page 21, "Borders—An Option." Select 5 or 10 mm size sequins of the same color as the design pieces for selected use. Refer to page 21, "Sequins and Gold Trim."

Step 5

Preshrink any washable fabrics that will be fused; make sure the grain is straight and iron out all wrinkles.

Step 6

Set up the work area. Lay out the cutting board, ironing board, iron, banner pattern, freezer wrap paper or paper-backed fusible web and other supplies listed in Step 3. Use a tote box for all of the smaller items.

Step 7

Prepare the background:

7.1 Cut out and hem the banner. If the fabric needs no interfacing to give it body, lay the piece on the cutting board wrong side up.

a. Use the cutting board grid and yard-sticks to mark the borders of the banner with tailor's chalk or pencil.

b. Allow 3 extra inches at the top for the dowel. If hems are to be used allow 1 inch for each side and 2 inches for the bottom.

c. Cut with scissors or a cutting wheel, metal ruler, and cutting pad. Use the grid (lines) as a guideline for ironing the hems on the cutting board.

d. Glue the hems in this order: sides, bottom, top. Apply the glue within ¼ inch of the edge and gently press into place. Leave side openings on the top and bottom hems for insertion of dowels when needed. Let the glue dry or set up before moving the banner.

e. If the side is not hemmed and the raw edge is fraying, place some glue on your fingertip and carefully run it along the back side of the cut edge to seal off any loose threads.

f. Turn the banner to the front side and align the edges with the grid on the cutting board.

7.2 If the fabric needs more body try the following options:

a. Use a dowel in the lower hem.

b. Glue the fabric to itself or other fabric. Refer to page 14, Solution 3.

c. Sandwich fusible web between two pieces of the same fabric and fuse. Refer to page 14, Solution 5.

d. Use fusible interfacing. Refer to page 15, Solutions 6 and 7.

*At this point continue with Steps 8 to 14 **if using glue for attaching the pieces to the background.** If using paper-backed fusible web for adhering the pieces to the background, continue with Step 15.*

Step 8

Trace the pattern pieces:

8.1 Use a black permanent marker to trace the design pieces from the banner's pattern to another piece of white freezer wrap paper. The traced line should be thin rather than wide; therefore, the marker should have a pointed tip rather than a wide or chisel tip.

8.2 Cut each paper design piece, leaving an outside margin or border ¼ to ½ inch in width.

Step 9

Prepare the background for the arrangement of design pieces: Position the banner's paper pattern over the background fabric and fuse according to the information on page 16, "Directions for Using Freezer Wrap Paper" and "Directions for Fusing the Banner Pattern to the Background."

Step 10

Prepare the design pieces:

10.1 Turn the iron to medium low heat and *no steam.*

10.2 Arrange the cut freezer wrap paper design pieces on the right side of the fabric. Be sure the paper's shiny side is facing down.

NOTE: If the fabric has a nap then lay all pieces in the same vertical direction as they would lay on the banner.

10.3 Glide the iron very quickly and without pressure over the paper. The polycoated side of the paper will adhere to the fabric. Practice with samples first. Refer to page 16, "Directions for Using Freezer Wrap Paper."

10.4 Cut out the design piece on the outside edge of the line so the *thin tracing line* can still be seen.

Step 11

Position the design pieces on the background:

11.1 After each design piece is cut, slip it immediately into position between the banner's pattern and the background. The paper of the banner pattern is transparent enough to see the cut pieces below so they can be moved into their exact position. *NOTE: The marker outlines on the design pieces will not show against a dark background, but the light portion can easily be seen.*

11.2 Continue until all pieces are in position.

> *NOTE: This method of placement cannot be used with brown freezer wrap paper. A yardstick is then used to determine where everything is to be placed by measuring distances from the edges and other pieces on the brown pattern. Use the cutting board's grid to assist in measuring on the background with the yardstick.*

Step 12

Arrange the letters and words:

12.1 Slip the yardstick between the banner's pattern and the background. Align the ruler horizontally and vertically with the grid and the row of wording on the pattern. Use ball head pins to secure both ends of the yardstick. Refer to page 16, "Illustration for Using the Cutting Board."

12.2 Place the letters along the edge of the ruler. Roll back the banner's pattern just enough to see the rectangles for placing each word.

12.3 To make sure a letter is not slanting, lay the plastic square on the yardstick next to the letter. Align the letter with the square.

12.3 Proofread for errors. Quickly, casually lay out the rest of the words for the other rows as a double check that there is sufficient spacing. Make any adjustments *before* gluing anything!

12.4 Before gluing the row of words, stick a couple of pins in the bottom part of each letter to hold it in place while gluing the top half. Refer to page 17, "Directions for Gluing."

12.5 Use a glue stick to slide glue under each letter or lift the top half of the letter and squeeze glue onto the back side of the letter. Gently press into place.

12.6 Glue the bottom half of each letter; then remove the yardstick and all the pins.

12.7 *Do not remove* the freezer paper pattern from the letters until the glue has thoroughly dried!

12.8 Continue with the next row of words.

Step 13

Make final adjustments before gluing design pieces:

13.1 Before the banner's pattern is gently removed, double-check the lines of any design piece (e.g., that the beams of the cross are in perfect vertical/horizontal alignment). Refer to page 16 for "Illustration for Using the Cutting Board."

13.2 Glue gold trim or a strand of sequins to a black felt strip before gluing the trim to the banner. Refer to page 18 for "Directions for Applying Felt Strips" and page 21 for "Sequins and Gold Trim."

13.3 Arrange and glue any ribbon or trim for the border. Refer to page 21 for "Borders—An Option."

13.4 Arrange and attach any 5 or 10 mm sequins with a Post-It brand glue stick (so the sequins can be moved about the banner) or use glue. Refer to page 21 for "Sequins and Gold Trim."

13.5 Use a few pins vertically stuck into each design piece to keep it from shifting while being glued.

Step 14

Glue all design pieces on the banner:

14.1 Glue each piece by running a thin line of glue just inside the cut edge on the back side. Wipe away blobs of glue that might ooze beyond the edge. If any pieces overlap, glue the bottom piece first. Refer to page 17 for "Directions for Gluing."

14.2 Allow the glue to set up or dry *before* removing the pins and the freezer wrap paper on the design pieces.

14.3 Continue with Step 16.

Step 15

Bonding with paper-backed fusible web is an alternative to using glue. Fused letters will not fray. Do test samples. Directions are as follows:

15.1 The design and lettering must be traced in reverse. Tape the paper banner pattern to a window and trace the lines of the design pieces and/or letters onto the paper side of paper-backed fusible web. *NOTE: Use heavy pencil lines or a permanent marker.* Do a test sample to check for any marker stains when using a steam iron.

15.2 Cut out the fusible paper patterns so there is a ¼-inch border or margin beyond the traced lines.

15.3 Place the paper/web design pattern (drawing side up) onto the back side of the fabric (to take into account any nap) and press according to the manufacturer's directions.

15.4 Remove the paper backing and position the piece or letter on the banner. Refer to page 16 for "Illustration for Using the Cutting Board" and review Steps 9, 11, 12, and 13 for positioning the pieces.

15.5 Double-check the arrangement and proofread the wording.

15.6 Carefully lay a press cloth over the pieces and fuse by ironing according to the manufacturer's directions. Shift the background so no fusing is done where there is a crease on the cutting board. Another option is to slip a wool-covered plywood board between the background and the cutting board and then fuse.

15.7 Arrange and attach any borders, fringe, or sequins. Refer to page 21, "Borders—An Option," and page 21, "Sequins and Gold Trim."

Step 16

Outline all the design pieces with narrow strips of black felt unless indicated otherwise for the banner. Refer to page 18, "Directions for Applying Felt Strips."

16.1 Glue each strip along the very outside cut edge of each piece, carefully stretching or bending the felt to match curves.
Square off all the corners. If the design ends in a V-shape then trim the felt into a matching V as well.

16.2 Refer to page 19 for "Directions for Applying Felt Strips as the Design Line" for designs such as on Banners 34–67.

16.3 Refer to page 20, "Yarn, an Alternative to Felt Strips."

Step 17

Preparation of the dowel and cord:

17.1 Measure and cut the wooden dowel so that it is ¼ to ½ inch longer than the finished edge of the banner.

17.2 Insert nails or eye screws in the ends of the dowel. Refer to the next section on "Dowels and Cords."

17.3 Attach the cord or link chain to one end of the dowel, insert the dowel through the hem at the top of the banner, then attach the cord or chain to the other end of the dowel.

17.4 The banner is ready to hang.

17.5 If the banner does not have enough body to hang without ripples, sags, or curling of the sides, insert a dowel in the bottom hem. Be sure the ends of the dowel do not protrude beyond the edge of the banner.

DOWELS AND CORDS

FISHERMAN'S KNOT

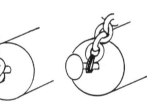

SIMPLE KNOT

WIRE CHAIN TO THE NAIL

CONNECT CORDS OR CHAINS TO THE EYESCREWS

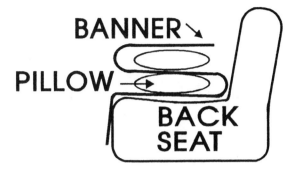

BANNER

PILLOW

BACK SEAT

TRANSPORTING YOUR BANNER

For transporting the banner to the church without wrinkling the fabric:

1. Drape the bottom edge of the banner over the edge of the car's back seat and across the seat. Lay a pillow on that portion of the banner. Drape the next part of the banner over the pillow and place another pillow on top of this. Again fold the remaining portion of the banner across the pillow. Continue the process. No creases will form on the banner. King-size pillows are best to use for large banners.

2. Reverse the sequence of Step 1 and remove the banner from the car.

3. Either hang the banner immediately or lay it flat on the floor until it can be hung.

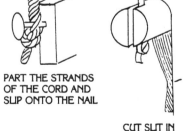

PART THE STRANDS OF THE CORD AND SLIP ONTO THE NAIL

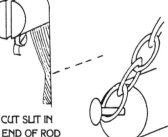

CUT SLIT IN END OF ROD

HOOK THE CHAIN OVER THE NAIL

For transporting a banner long distance by plane, mail, or car:

1. Sandwich the banner between two layers of soft, thick, quilted fabric that are cut a little wider than the banner. The bottom layer should be 2 feet longer than the banner.

2. Place a cardboard roll at the top edge where all three fabrics meet together. Use wide packing tape to hold the bottom quilted layer to the cardboard tube. Gently roll up the fabrics.

3. Use packing tape to secure the roll. The dowel and cord can be tucked into the center of the cardboard roll. Close off the ends of the roll with tape, or use a scrap of cloth stretched over the end of the roll and a rubber band to secure the piece. Do not allow the rubber band to constrict the banner.

4. The roll will travel well in the car, but should not have other items pushing against it or on it.

5. For air transport or mail, place the roll in a long narrow carton and ship. A home-made carton may be cut to size.

STORAGE OF BANNERS

Banners should be stored in an area without sunlight. Windows should be covered with shades that do not permit sunlight into the room. The banners can be hung from wall brackets mounted approximately 60 inches apart and close to the ceiling, or on hooks that hang from a bar that is mounted to the ceiling. Store the banners facing the wall. Drape a cloth across the top of the banners to catch the dust. Remove and shake the dust out of the cloth from time to time. Make a pole with a hook on the end as an aid in reaching the nail or hook on which the banner is to be mounted or removed.

WALL BRACKET

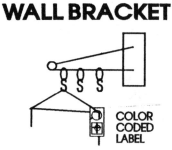

COLOR CODED LABEL

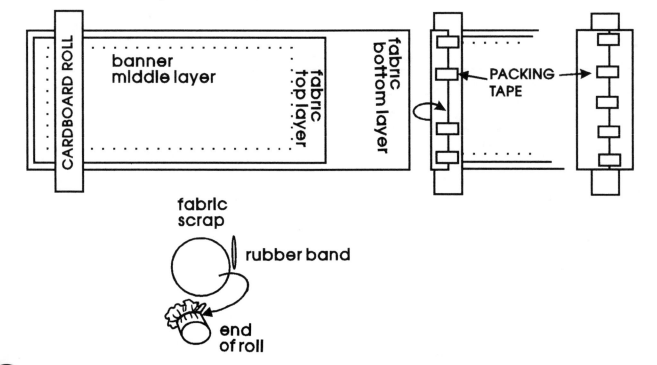

CARDBOARD ROLL

banner middle layer

fabric top layer

fabric bottom layer

PACKING TAPE

fabric scrap

rubber band

end of roll

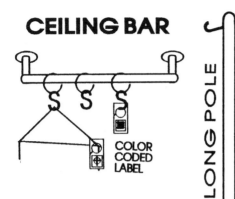

CEILING BAR

LONG POLE

COLOR
CODED
LABEL

Proper labeling and record keeping is crucial when storing banners. Each banner should have a self-stick label in the lower right corner on the back side with the following information:

Season (if applicable)

Church Year Series A, B, or C (if applicable)

Sunday or special occasion or theme

Date when the banner was made

Name of person(s) who made the banner

A copy of the design or a photo along with the information on the back of the banner should be kept in a loose-leaf notebook that has color-coded section dividers listing the church seasons, special Sundays, special occasions, or themes. The banners should be stored in the same order as the color-coded sections in the notebook.

Make color-coded cards that correspond to the sections in the notebook and are labeled with the season or special use. Glue a copy of the banner's design to the card for easy identification. Hang the card

on the end of the cord where it attaches to the rod. All banners should have the cards attached on the same left or right side. When removing the banner from storage, hang the card on the wall bracket or bar in the same place where the banner was hanging. This makes it easy to locate and place the banner back into the same place in storage.

Color coded label

COMMON PROBLEMS AND THEIR SOLUTIONS

This section will alert the banner maker to potential problems and offer solutions so the banner can be made with less trouble. The three major difficulties come from moisture, the steam iron, and the choice of materials.

Moisture

Problem. Fusing with a steam iron can cause wrinkles, warping, or puckering in the two fabrics. The steam can cause shrinkage in a fabric that is not preshrunk, is moisture sensitive, or shrinks differently than the fabric to which it is fused.

Solution 1. Use fabrics that do not require fusible interfacing to give the background body. Try upholstery fabrics, thermal-lined (rubber-like substance) drapery, fabrics with a stretch-retardant backing, heavy drapes, cottons and blends (duck cloth, denim), corduroy (only if glue is used with this fabric, as ironing will ruin the nap), and Ultrasuede (purchase only when on sale!).

> *NOTE: Ultrasuede must be ironed on a wool-covered board under a press cloth or the nap will be ruined or the imprint of the bottom of the iron or steam holes will show.*

Thermal-lined drapery is a favorite and comes in both cotton- and satin-type finishes.

Solution 2. If the fabric needs more body, first try using a dowel in the lower hem. It would be best to hem the sides as added reinforcement against stretching out of shape along the edge. This will not solve the stretching problems of felt.

Solution 3. This is the easiest and least expensive way to line a banner. I suggest using this method for satin and similar fabrics. Lay two pieces of the same fabric with wrong sides together on the cutting board. Push a few pins straight down through the fabrics into the cutting board somewhere near the banner edges of the material so it does not shift. Use the grid on the cutting board as a guide to measure, mark, and cut the banner to size, allowing an extra 3 inches at the top for the dowel hem. No other hems are needed. Starting at the top of the banner, lay back the top fabric piece about 8 inches from the top edge. Run a line of glue just above the 6-inch line on the bottom fabric piece. If the fabric is transparent enough, use the grid line on the cutting board as a guide for gluing. If not, lay down a yardstick as a guide. Fold the top piece back into place and let the glue dry. Gently lift the side edge of the top piece and run a thin line of glue along the edge of the bottom fabric. (Be careful not to glue along the top 6 inches of the side.) Gently pat the top piece into place. Let the glue dry. Finish the other side and the bottom in the same way. Make the top hem by folding down the top edge of the banner 3 inches and applying glue within ¼ inch of the edge. Fold the top piece back into place and press firmly. DO NOT glue the sides of the top hem or else the dowel can not be inserted. Allow the glue to dry. Secure any fraying by running a thin line of glue with your fingertip along the back side of the cut edge.

Solution 4. Use a Lotus or Elna press, which uses heat and pressure only. The press is excellent for fusing and ironing without the use of moisture. Ask around to locate a seamstress or tailor who owns one.

Solution 5. The following method is more expensive but will provide consistently better results than using a fusible interfacing. Sandwich fusible web between two panels of the same fabric. The panels of the fusible web should overlap slightly. The fusing must be done over the entire surface or the fabric will bulge where it is not fused. Do a test sample. Any shrinkage caused by the steam iron will be the same for both panels and not cause unsightly puckering or warping. After the fusing is done, cut the banner to the exact size, allowing for the 3-inch hem at the top for the rod. No other hems are needed.

> *WARNING: Be careful not to iron directly onto the fusible web. It will severely gum up the surface of the iron and only fine steel wool will remove the melted material.*

An appliqué nonstick pressing sheet will protect the iron and the ironing surface from being gummed by the webbing. The sheet will also allow fusible web to be fused to the back side of a fabric piece, which then can be fused to the banner background. Letters cut from fabric prepared this way will not fray. This pressing sheet is a space-age plastic film found at fabric stores or mail order: Nancy's Notions, P.O. Box 683, Beaver Dam, WI 53916-0683.

Solution 6. Use a fusible interfacing with background fabrics such as felt or material that tends to sag, stretch out of shape, or curl along the edges. It is tricky to fuse two panels of interfacing to the background so the front side does not have puckering or ridges. Abut the two edges of the interfacing panels so there is no overlapping or gaps, then fuse according to manufacturer's directions. Practice with scraps.

Solution 7. Preshrink both the fabric and the fusible interfacing. Carefully dip the lining in a bathtub containing very warm water. Let the material drip-dry someplace where it will not form creases or wrinkles.

Solution 8. A felt background needs fusible interfacing, but some felt does not fuse without problems. When a felt banner is small, (e.g., 2 feet by 2 feet), place clear packing tape on the back side of the felt along each of the four sides. Gently tap the tape in place so there is no puckering or stretching along the edges. Do a practice piece first to see if the results are satisfactory.

Pressing with a Steam Iron

Problem. Shiny spots, water spots, and imprints from the iron or steam vents might show when fusing. A stained or soiled ironing board cover will stain light-colored fabrics.

Solution 1. Drape a clean white cloth or bedsheet over the ironing board before ironing if the board's cover is stained.

Solution 2. Use a press cloth and a hard, smooth surface or a wool-covered board and a clean iron.

Solution 3. Use a synthetic fiber press cloth and cover the ironing surface with the same when ironing nylon fabric. Nylon attracts cotton and wool fibers and will look

messy after it is ironed.

Solution 4. Attach a nonstick plate to the pressing surface of the iron. These attach by a spring to the iron and have tiny holes for the steam vents. This eliminates shiny marks and may lessen the imprints of the iron and its steam holes.

Solution 5. Avoid water marks on some delicate fabrics by using the proper steam settings on an iron. Also keep the iron meticulously clean.

Solution 6. Use an Elna or Lotus press for ironing.

Solution 7. Avoid having wrinkles put in the fabric when purchasing the material. This will save so much time and work later on! Fabrics with a nap (velvets, corduroy) and delicate fabrics (satins) are difficult to iron once creased or wrinkled. Do not allow the sales clerk or cashier to fold up the fabric once it is cut. Have it rolled onto a cardboard roll. Purchase empty ones if necessary. The fabric can be hand rolled and held by the end. Smile politely and explain how this saves ironing time when making a banner.

Choosing Materials

Problem. Fabrics that must be lined.

Solution. Light-colored or white design pieces should be lined with white or the same colored fabric to keep the color vibrant when glued to a dark background. Light-colored pieces can be glued to the same fabric or to white fabric. Before cutting out the design piece, pin it to the white or same-colored fabric. Cut both fabrics at the same time and glue the two pieces together along the edge before placing it on the background.

Sandwich fusible web between two pieces of same-colored fabric and fuse according to directions. The fused piece is now ready for the paper pattern, cutting, and gluing.

Problem. Some fabrics should *not* be preshrunk.

Things to Remember. Some fabrics lose their "new" look when washed. Polished cotton loses its sheen. Corduroy loses its crisp look and it becomes difficult to press the nap to make it look as good as new. Felt varies in its fiber content and may shrink severely.

Problem. Some fabrics are *not suited* for banners.

Things to Remember. Avoid using the following: fabric that is too lightweight to beinterfaced; fabric that does not glue or bond easily or is too sensitive to moisture; dull or grayed colors; knits (too stretchy), and gold that is not highly reflective. Velvet is not suitable for banner backgrounds because the nap is too deep for bonding pieces or strips. Fusible interfacing could be used to stabilize velour knits.

TIPS AND HOW-TOS

Directions for Using Freezer Wrap Paper

Ideally the fusing of freezer wrap paper to fabric will make it possible to cut out letters and design pieces with great speed and ease. The process will keep the more delicate parts of a design piece from shifting or stretching out of shape before the piece is glued into place.

Practice fusing freezer wrap paper to various kinds of fabric. Try a medium-low heat with *no steam*. Experiment to see what temperature on your iron works best, how long to keep the iron on the paper, and the amount of pressure to use. *A quick, light swipe of the iron is all that is needed.* Test to see how easily the paper will come off the fabric once it is cooled. If

the paper is over-fused on loose fiber fabric, such as felt, the paper will not peel off without wrecking the fabric. When the paper cools, it will more easily pop off of hard, smooth-finish fabric such as satin. If the paper does pop off, it can be ironed back on if needed.

Directions for Fusing the Banner Pattern to the Background

A real time-saver is to use the banner's paper pattern as a guideline for arranging the pieces and words. Place the paper pattern on top of the banner and fuse it so it will not slip out of position. Fuse areas of the pattern where there are no words or design pieces, most likely at the 3–6 inch top or bottom portions of the pattern. Be careful not to fuse the pattern to any pieces laying on the background. Refer to the illustration below. This fusing allows the rest of the pattern to be lifted or rolled back where needed for placement of pieces and words. *NOTE: Fused portions of the paper pattern can be pulled up and re-fused as many times as needed and wherever needed!*

If you are unable to find white freezer

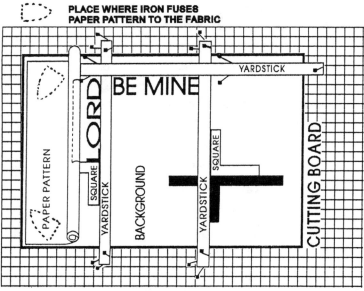

Illustration for Using the Cutting Board

wrap paper with the polycoated side, write to Reynolds Metals Company—Consumer Products Division; P.O. Box 85583; Richmond, VA 23285-5583.

Directions for Gluing

Three Methods for Gluing Design Pieces

Always use a thick tacky craft glue. This kind of glue has less moisture and will cause less bleeding and shrinkage of the fabric. *NOTE: Words and design pieces should be arranged and glued or fused in place* **before** *gluing any felt strips.* Gluing may be done in any of the following ways:

Method 1. Form a continuous thin line of glue by gently squeezing the bottle while moving the tip within ¼ inch of the edge on the back side of the piece. Gently press the pieces in place. Check for bleeding. *NOTE: Blobs formed by the glue can bleed to the surface of thinner fabrics and will leave a shiny spot or discoloration. Avoid this by spreading the glue very thin or by spreading out any blobs that form.*

Method 2. Use the tip of your finger or a cotton swab dipped into glue that has been squeezed into the cap of a 2-liter bottle. Spread the glue along the edge of the back side of the piece.

Method 3. In this method the parts of the design pieces never have to be lifted off the surface of the banner in order to apply the glue. The glue is applied to a homemade cardboard stick and slipped in under the edge and moved along under the edge until the glue is gone. Then reglue the applicator and continue the procedure. Gently pat down the edge. If there is a buildup of fibers and bits of lumpy glue on the tip of the applicator, wipe it clean with a paper towel.

METHOD 1

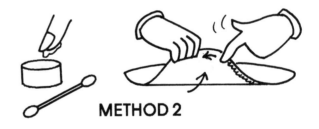

METHOD 2

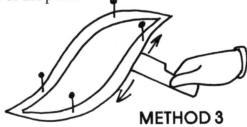

METHOD 3

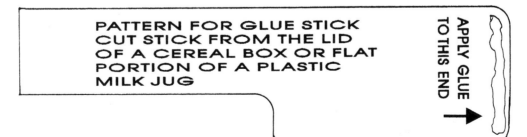

PATTERN FOR GLUE STICK
CUT STICK FROM THE LID
OF A CEREAL BOX OR FLAT
PORTION OF A PLASTIC
MILK JUG

APPLY GLUE
TO THIS END →

Directions for Applying Felt Strips

The banner is almost completed once the gluing and/or fusing of the ribbons, fringes, design pieces, and letters are done. The remaining touch is what makes the banner and all its colors come alive, providing the dignity and grandeur of the stained-glass windows of cathedrals. Each design piece of the banner is now outlined with ¼-inch black felt strips (unless otherwise indicated on the banner pattern). Letters should not be outlined.

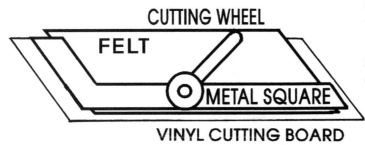

Cutting the Strips

Place black felt fabric onto a vinyl cutting pad. Use a carpenter's square with the cutting wheel. While holding the square firmly with one hand, move the cutting wheel along the metal edge of the square until you come to the edge of the vinyl pad. Carefully lift and move the square over ¼ inch or the desired width and cut another strip. *Note: Usually you can eyeball the width to match the previous one without having to measure for each strip. If not, then cut a strip of paper the desired width and lay it on the felt as a visual measurement. Check that the width is the same for both ends of the strip before cutting.*

Continue cutting the strips until there are enough to outline all of the pieces on the banner. To save time and energy for future banners cut ½ yard or more of soft black felt into strips. If some strips are wider than others, then sort the strips into two or three groups according to width. Use the same width of strips for completing an outline on

a design piece. Store the unused strips in a box or on a hanger for use on later banners.

Gluing the Strips

Run a thin line of glue next to, but not on the cut edge of the design piece. Place the felt strip adjacent to the cut edge. Gently push and stretch the felt around curves. If space is a premium, then glue the strip directly over the cut edge or just inside of it on the design piece. To secure metallic pieces that may not stick with glue, run the line of glue so it is on *both* the metallic piece and the background, then center the strip on the cut edge.

To attach the next strip, trim the end of it at an angle and overlap it slightly onto the end of the preceding strip. Use a dot of glue so the angled tip does not hang loose. Extra

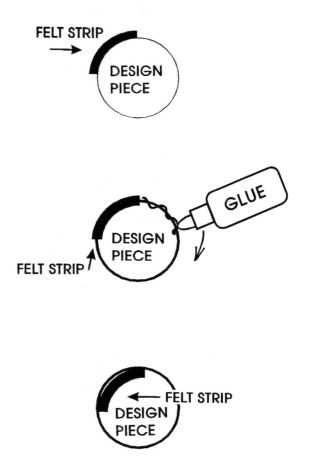

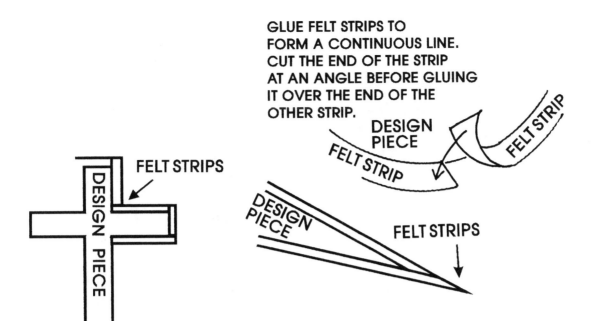

GLUE FELT STRIPS TO
FORM A CONTINUOUS LINE.
CUT THE END OF THE STRIP
AT AN ANGLE BEFORE GLUING
IT OVER THE END OF THE
OTHER STRIP.

trimming may be needed on the end of a strip if it is slightly larger in width than the preceding one. Square off corners at a right angle as on the outside or inside corners of a cross. Corners that are formed by other angles should be trimmed to match the same shaped angle.

Wider strips must be made of *soft* felt to insure the stretching qualities needed. Use your fingers to gently stretch the outside edge of the strip for curves. The inside curve line of the strip will pucker. Cut ½-inch long slits where the edge puckers. Press it flat with your fingers and the slits will form small wedges conforming the strip to the curve line. Glue in place.

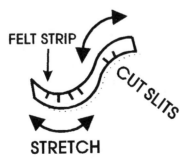

Directions for Applying Felt Strips As the Design Line

Some banners use felt strips for the design line itself and not just for outlining design pieces. The two ways to apply the strips accurately are as follows:

Method 1. Use a tracing wheel and tracing paper suitable for fabric to transfer the design to the background. First fuse the banner pattern to the background in a couple of corners so the paper will not shift. Refer to page 16, "Directions for Fusing the Banner Pattern to the Background." Trace the lines. Remove the banner pattern and glue the strips onto the traced lines. Use a yardstick pinned to the cutting board as a guide for gluing long, straight lines. About the strip next to the ruler's edge. The strip will look perfectly straight and even. If help is needed for forming smooth curves, use a Flexcurv bent to the shape of the curve or use plates and lids. The hard edge on these items has the same function as the yardstick's edge—it provides a firm base against which to nudge or abut the felt. Most likely the only item your will need is the yardstick.

Method 2. Fuse the banner pattern to the background in the area where the

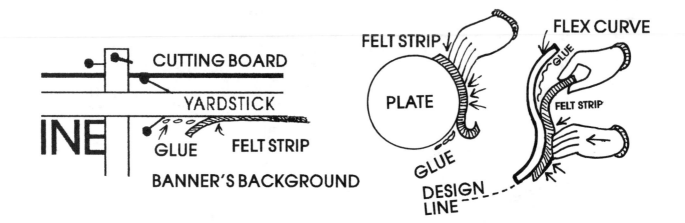

design lines are located. Refer to page 16, "Directions for Fusing the Banner Pattern to the Background." *NOTE: All design pieces and wording, if any, should be already glued in place before any cutting of the paper pattern begins.* Starting with the outermost lines, cut along the line on the paper. Gently lift away and pin down the portion of paper just enough so a felt strip can be glued along the cut line on the paper pattern. Continue line by line on the pattern until all the lines have been glued. It is faster to pin the yardstick on the straight lines and then glue the strip than to glue along the paper line itself. The Flexcurv may be used for curves. Use whatever works the fastest with the best results.

Yarn—An Alternative to Felt Strips

Black rug yarn is an alternative to felt strips. It is thinner than felt and easy to apply, though the texture and appearance will be different than that of felt. Check that the yarn will hold with glue. Prepare the yarn by ironing it free of wrinkles. Use a steam iron on medium setting and slowly pull the yarn under the iron. Make a blunt cut on the end of the yarn and dip it into some glue. If necessary, use a finger to press the end if the fibers are spreading apart. Let it dry. This will keep the cut end from fraying. *NOTE: Remember to do the same for the end of the yarn piece where it finally meets and is glued to the beginning portion.*

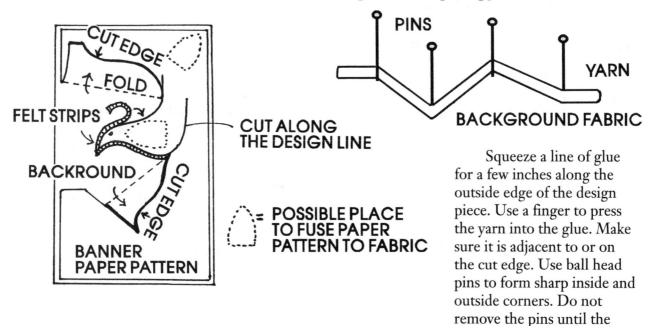

Squeeze a line of glue for a few inches along the outside edge of the design piece. Use a finger to press the yarn into the glue. Make sure it is adjacent to or on the cut edge. Use ball head pins to form sharp inside and outside corners. Do not remove the pins until the glue dries.

Borders—An Option

There is room for borders on most designs in this book. Borders are optional and are unnecessary if a ban is used on the same dowel. Place ribbon on the edge if there is little contrast between the banner's background and the wall. Experiment with borders. Select one of the design's colors or its complementary color. Try different combinations by placing ribbon on one or both sides, with or without the bottom or top edges. The bulk of the dowel makes it awkward to place ribbon so it nicely frames the top of the banner. More than one color and width of ribbon may be used at varying distances from the edge.

Sequins and Gold Trim

Purchase a variety of colors of 5 and 10 mm sequins from a craft or fabric store. Banners 94, 137, and 204 use white iridescent sequins as stars. Banners 203 and 217 use sequins to add sparkle to parts of the design. Sequins should match the color of the design piece. Stars made of iridescent white sequins appear as glittery dots. The sequins may also be the same color as the background (the sparkles will suggest the twinkling light of stars). Try both and decide which looks best for the overall design from a distance.

One to three sequins can add a glint to the bottom corner of a leaf, base of a flame, the reflection of a grape or wings of an angel. Place a green sequin on a globe piece to indicate where your church is located. Use sequins to form simple lines or designs on a crown. Use a Post-It brand glue stick to apply a layer of glue to the back side of a sequin. Let the glue set up for 30 minutes before sticking the sequin to the banner. The sequins can be repositioned many times and stored on paper when not needed. If the banner is to be transported the sequins may need to be glued permanently.

A strand of sequins (5 or 10 mm in size) or any gold trim is aesthetically more appealing when glued onto a black ribbon or felt strip with 3⁄16 to 1⁄4 inch margin on each side. This is optional. The black provides greater contrast with the background, unless the background is already black or dark. *NOTE: Most ribbon will not bend on curves, but felt will.*

The width of highly reflective gold trim may be dependent on what is available. For example, Banners 18 and 24 have a large open area that allows for wider trim than the small confined area within the Baptism shell of Banner 157. Take the banner pattern to the store to more easily select the appropriate width by laying the trim on the pattern.

BANS (MINIBANNERS)

The Creative Use of Bans

Bans are minibanners that are long and narrow and contain either a message, name, symbol, design, or a combination of these. Here are six different ways to feature bans:

1. Bans Used Individually

A ban may be made and displayed alone. Bans are easy but meaningful gifts for Baptism, confirmations, weddings, anniversaries, special recognitions, or any other special theme. Select any symbol or design from the patterns given in this book to create a ban that will fit any occasion. Enlarge and use the alphabet patterns for the wording.

2. Bans Used in Addition to a Banner

Display a confirmation banner. Make individual bans for each confirmand with his or her name along with the symbol of a cross or dove. The doves of Bans 125–133 or a dove from any banner could be placed near the top. Group the bans attractively in relationship to the banner. Later, give the bans as gifts to the confirmands. The same could be done with a Baptism ban such as Bans 152 and 156, which contain a dove or shell/cross symbol and the name of the baptismal candidate.

3. Bans Used As a Group

Bans for a season or with a particular theme can be displayed all at the same time as a group (e.g., the Advent Series Banners 11–14; Banners 125–133 for "Fruit of the Spirit"; Banners 88–90 or Banner 92 for Trinity Sunday).

4. Bans That Accumulate Week by Week

In a series of bans (e.g., the Advent Series Banners 1–4, Banner 9, the Advent Series Banners 11–14), the first ban is hung on the first Sunday, the second ban is added to the first one on the second Sunday. Continue until all the bans in the series are displayed.

5. Bans That Weekly Feature a Portion of a Series

Use a banner for a series of sermons for a particular season, such as Lent (e.g., Banner 70). Each week a new ban is hung on the dowel with the banner. The new ban features a different text or emphasis for that theme. An option is to display the used bans in another area within the church as an arranged grouping or spaced out individually throughout the nave.

6. Bans Extend the Life of a Banner

Prepare a banner design without any wording (e.g., Banner 102). The emphasis of the banner can be changed by using different bans. The color of each new ban could match the season or one of the colors in the design.

For example, you could remove the word *alleluia* from Banner 74. Place the ban on the dowel alongside the banner or hang it separately. Use wording such as the following:

Easter—"He Is Risen"

Funeral—"Heaven Is My Home"
Lord's Prayer—"Deliver Us from Evil"
Christian Life—"Alive in Christ"
  "Freedom"
  "Freedom in Christ"
  "Your Faith Has Set You Free"
  "God's Promises Are Sure"

Alternative wording for bans is offered for some of the banners in this book. Readjust the size of the banner or the placement of the design if words are removed from a banner design. Any number of bans can then be used with that particular banner.

Directions for Making a Ban

Bans can range in width from approximately 7 to 18 inches. The length will vary according to the space needed for a name, message, or symbol or the length of a matching banner. If the ban is handled sparingly, unlined heavy felt may be used. Use a strong straw like the ones found in fast food restaurants as a dowel for a ban up to 36 inches in length. Cut the width of the ban to fit the length of the straw, usually 7½ inches. Use dental floss for the cord. A hairpin makes an excellent needle for stringing the floss through the straw. Pull the tied portion of the cord to the inside of the straw out of view. Ideas for the placement of words are shown on the bans' designs throughout the book. If necessary, make ½- to 1-inch hems using glue or fuse with a roll of fusible web. Heavy fabrics can have raw edges.

Bans used with a large banner are cut to match the length of the banner. If using a single line of wording with 3-inch high

letters, then cut the ban approximately 7 inches wide. If two lines of wording are used then make the ban approximately 11 inches wide. The color of the ban should match or be complementary to the colors on the banner or should match the season.

Double-Stick Tape and Post-It Brand Glue Stick

Design pieces, sequins, and words may be attached, removed, or repositioned on a banner or ban by using double-stick tape. An example of this use is the Passion Series Banners 29–33. The cross, crown, and halo are permanently attached to the banner. For each service the wording and a new symbol are attached with double-stick tape. The pieces are carefully removed to keep the tape attached to them and are then stored on sheets of waxed paper until used again.

Thus letters from the same alphabet set may be used repeatedly on the same banner or on other banners and bans. Use pressure to stick letters to a hard, smooth-finish fabric to make sure the letters won't fall off in the middle of a service.

Adhesive from a repositional glue stick (such as Post-It brand) may be applied to the back of letters that do not fray easily. Apply the glue stick before removing the freezer wrap paper to keep the fabric from stretching out of shape. The letters are reusable and may be stored on notebook paper in a binder when not in use. If in doubt use double-stick tape. The glue stick may also be used to bond sequins if the banner is not being transported. Be sure there is enough glue sticking to the back side of each sequin. Experiment and see what happens.

ARRANGING WORDS

Note how the words are arranged on the banners:

Direction

a. Words begin on the bottom and go up the left side.

b. Words go across the top from left to right.

c. Words on the right side begin at the top corner and continue toward the bottom.

Wording going up can symbolize the human response to God. Wording that goes down from the top could symbolize God's interaction with us.

Arrangement

a. Several rows of words may have left or right margins or both.

b. Wording may fit in an area of an imaginary square, rectangle, oval, triangle, or circle.

c. The width of the capital letter *O* is used for spacing between words; if space is tight use the letter *E*.

TOY COY LOV IOI SER

Spacing

Leave at least 2 to 3 inches between the design pieces and the words. Borders or empty space between the farthest extension of the design and wording to the side of the banner is established in this proportion:

SIDES—have the least space, about 3 inches

BOTTOM—has the most space, about 5 inches

TOP—has more space than the sides and less space than the bottom, approximately 4 inches

Rules for Letters

Letters should be at least 3 inches in height in order to be seen from a distance. The spacing

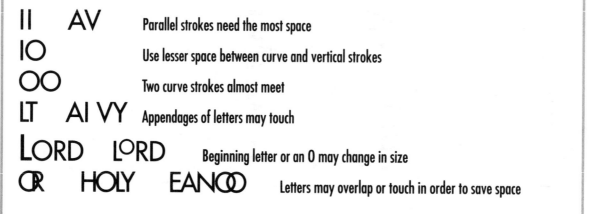

for letters is illustrated in progression from those needing the most space to those needing the least space.

ARRANGEMENT OF DESIGN AND USE OF COLOR

In creating a new banner design avoid having separate items float about on the banner; group items together or connect them by lines such as a cross (e.g., Banner 219), blocks, or strips of color. The eye should see the center of interest first and then travel around the rest of the banner and be led back to the center of interest. Those items outside the center of interest may form a triangle or an S shape (e.g., Banner 100) or zigzag like a Z that leads the eye into the central area from both ends. Items for the center of interest should be near the center, larger than other objects and be made of warmer or lighter colors than the rest.

The banner's colors should reflect the colors for the church year. Colors that are light, bright, and warm (yellow, red, orange) come forward. Dark and cool (blue, green, purple) colors recede.

Use light, bright colors. Limit the number of colors to no more than three plus black and white. Look at the color wheel. The complementary colors (colors opposite of each other on the color wheel) are more intense when used together: red-green, blue-orange, yellow-purple). A triangle combination would be red-blue-yellow and purple-orange-green. Another good combination is to select complementary colors (e.g., red and green) and for one of those colors (green) use the neighboring color on each side of it (yellow and blue).

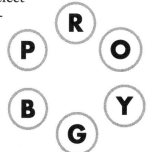

This combination can be used with other colors (e.g., yellow and purple plus the neighbors of yellow—orange and green.)

Markers and Watercolor Paints

Markers can provide a quick alternative to felt lines as well as fulfill the need for detailed coloring. A line drawn alongside a felt strip will enhance the angel's clothing and wings on Banner 18. An orange marker could be used to add color to the base of a yellow flame or enhance the lines of the flames on Banners 9 or 10.

The stems and leaves of the lilies for Banner 75 may be drawn with markers on a *white* satin background and even outlined with black markers, though felt strips provide a sharper image. *WARNING: One slip of the black marker while forming a line could ruin a whole banner.* Satin has a tooth to it that offers resistance to the marker when moving in one direction, but is very slick when going in the other direction. Practice on scraps.

If turquoise or lavender satin is used as the background for Banner 75, use a separate piece of satin fused to itself. If the background is dark then use light, bright green markers and if the background is light use deeper, darker green markers. The idea is to have a strong contrast between darks and lights. Black marker could be used for outlining the green because the design will be cut and glued to the background. Black felt strips would be more aesthetic than markers but would take more time. Watercolor paints bleed and are best used when painted freely on the fabric before the design is traced, cut, and glued. The leaves and stems of Banner 75 could be done on a separate piece of satin, outlined in black marker, cut out, and glued to the background. Black felt strips may be used instead of the marker. Do not try to color too large of an area with one color; there may not be enough paint in the watercolor tray's cup!

Banners 23, 108, 185, 210, and 214 have globes. (A globe can also be used in place of the yellow portions of Banner 82.) These are perfect for doing a watercolor wash of greens, oranges, and yellows for land areas and blue for oceans on satin fabric. The lines for land masses must be traced on the globe before painting begins. It is all right if the colors of ocean and land bleed into each other along the coastal boundaries. A marker could be used to draw lines for the land masses if so desired. Cut out the globe and it is ready to be glued to the background. The coloring process is so quick and easy! The shininess of the satin will remain intact through the watercolor. From a distance it looks fabulous! Refer also to the information in the "Directions for Painting a Watercolor Rainbow" that follow.

Markers and watercolor paints handle differently on thermal-lined drapery material with a cotton-like finish than on satin. The drapery fabric allows a more precise delineation. There is less bleeding. The colors will be bolder but flatter in appearance. This fabric is better suited for markers.

Marking lines freehand is scary; use a ruler for drawing straight lines and a cardboard circle or Flexcurv to help with curves. Do samples first!

WARNING: Banners, especially those colored by markers and watercolor paints, will fade if left in direct sunlight. The solution is to face the banner to the wall or remove it to a dark storage area after the church service or special occasion is over.

Directions for Painting a Watercolor Rainbow

Try this method on different kinds of satin scraps since fiber contents vary. Place satin over a paper pattern of a rainbow and very lightly pencil the arch lines. Use Crayola brand watercolor paints (single tray) and a 1-inch-wide soft brush. Tape freezer wrap paper, shiny side up, to a flat, smooth surface. Have 20 or so sheets of paper towels or napkins close by and two containers of water. Load the watercolor cups of the rainbow colors with water and let them soak a couple of minutes. Wet the brush. Place the satin piece on top of the freezer paper.

Load up the brush with **yellow** paint and brush it over the strip that is indicated for yellow. Work the yellow into the satin within the band's lines. Load the brush with more water to get more yellow on the brush. Continue spreading yellow on the marked band from one end of the band to the other. Yellow will bleed along the pencil lines into the adjoining bands. Let the yellow bleed no more than ½ inch across the lines.

Controlling the Bleeding: As the paint goes on it spreads beyond the brush strokes. To stop or control the spread, immediately grab and crumple a paper towel and wipe it across the yellow, especially in the area where the spreading is taking place. Just wipe across the whole surface where the brush has just been worked. It's all right to wipe into the next band. *This absorbs the excess yellow that is spreading.* Then lift the edge of the fabric and look to see where the excess yellow has accumulated on the freezer wrap paper. Quickly wipe up the excess paint with one or two swipes. Dip the brush into the water and swirl it in the color cup to get a rich mixture of color on the brush. Wipe as often as needed to keep from bleeding too much into the adjoining bands. Every time the top surface is wiped then immediately wipe up the excess moisture on the freezer paper below. This process goes as quickly as the paint can be applied and wiped.

Do the outer **red** band next. Clean the brush and get clean water before using the next color. Use clean paper towels for each new color. Use the same painting process. Since red is the outer band, the outside edge's bleeding does not have to be monitored because the satin will be cut on that line and glued in place on the banner. *The spread of red into the yellow must be controlled.* Take the brush up to the line but not over into the yellow. Each time the brush goes along the line, immediately grab a clean paper towel and first wipe the top of the satin, then quickly wipe the excess moisture underneath on the freezer wrap paper. If there is still bleeding wipe again. Apply just enough pressure when wiping the fabric's surface to absorb the excess moisture but not damage the fabric's fibers.

The next color is **green**. Apply it the same as the red along the yellow line. Do not let the green spread more than ½ inch into the band for the blue. Do the **blue** band next. Stop the spread beyond the line into the green and let the blue bleed ½ inch into the band for the purple. The last to apply is the **purple**. Do not worry about the bleeding to the outside; that line will be cut. Stop the spread of the purple at the line for the blue. The painting and wiping goes so fast that it's done in a few minutes. Wipe the underside dry. *NOTE: The key to controlling the bleeding and to keeping water marks from forming in the process of drying is to absorb the excess moisture on top of and below the fabric piece with paper towels. Ironing immediately with a warm, dry iron sets the colors before any water marks can form.*

The fabric rainbow may stretch from the wiping. It is best to lay the rainbow on top of the pattern and retrace the outside lines for cutting. Glue the rainbow of Banner 74 to the white butterfly. Lay the painted rainbow of Banner 215 on the pattern and mark it again for cutting. Position the rainbow on the white background and glue. Use black felt strips to outline only the outermost edge of the rainbow.

Experiment with this method until you feel confident with it. The colors will be somewhat pastel in appearance. Have extra fabric in case the results are not satisfactory. Do not throw away any rainbows. Use them to make minibanners for Sunday school. Use a marker to write a message on the rainbow, such as "God loves me!" or "God's promises are sure!" Children will love the colors even if the bands got a little wild in places. It will look beautiful! The rainbows can also be recycled as fabric book covers or tote bags for church organizations. Have some fun!

PART 2

Banner Designs

KEY TO THE DESIGNS (NUMBER AND COLOR CODE INFORMATION)

IMPORTANT! Read this page before purchasing materials for any of these banners!

Scale: ¼" in the book = 3" on the full-size design

Number Code

Numbers and letters on the banner design correspond to a color on the color key on the back cover.

One number or letter is used to indicate the color for all of the words on the banner. A *number or letter within a circle* indicates that word only has that particular color.

If a large design area such as the background is divided into smaller parts, do all in the same color.

All identical items, such as stars or small crosses, will have the same color, which will be indicated by one number or letter only.

- - - - indicates a line to be made by a colored marker (usually drawn next to the felt strip) or by flexible gold or other colored metallic trim (e.g., a strand of sequins or gold cording/ribbon).

B½ indicates the black line is approximately ½ inch wide.

* indicates the place to glue or stick a 5 or 10 mm sequin on the banner.

Letters stand for the following:

F = any choice of flesh color

L# = lighter shade of color for that number

D# = darker shade of color for that number

W = white

B = black

G = highly reflective, metallic gold

GB or **GW** = gold trim glued to a black (**GB**) or white (**GW**) felt strip (see p. 21, "Sequins and Gold Trim")

S = sequin

S# = color of the sequin

B/W or ⅔ = there is a choice of two colors; the first choice is the first number or letter

Add fringe, trim, or ribbon to the sides and/or bottom of the banner designs as desired.

A color scheme other than the one indicated may be used. Use crayons or markers to color copies of the design until the most attractive combination is reached.

If an overhead projector is not available for enlarging patterns, then make a transparency of the grid on page 4. Paper clip the grid to the design to be enlarged. Measure and cut the pattern to size. Use the grid on your cutting board as a guide for marking 3-inch squares on the paper pattern. Enlarge the design square by square.

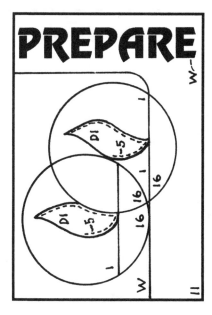

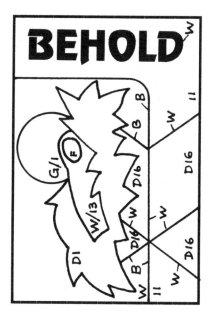

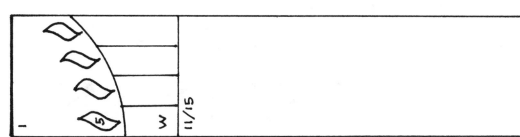

Advent

Banners 1–4 (Advent Set)

36" × 24"

Read "Bans That Accumulate Week by Week,"
page 22.

Advent 1—A: Watch
(Matt. 24:42); B: Peace
(1 Cor.1:3); C: Come
(1 Thess. 3:13)

Advent 2—A, B, C:
Prepare (A: Matt.
11:10; B: Is. 40:3;
C: Mal. 3:1)

Advent 3—A, B, C:
Rejoice (B: Luke 1:47;
C: Zeph. 3:14)

Advent 4—A: Glory
(Ps. 24:7–10); Jesus
(Matt. 1:21); B: Behold
(Luke 1:31 KJV); C: Joy
(Is. 12:6)

Use double-stick tape for
the letters.

Advent

Banner 5

9" × 48"

Options: Leave as is or
add any flame design to
the upper area.

Advent

Banner 6

15" × 72"

Options: Quote a portion
of Scripture for each
Advent Sunday; change
the wording weekly
using double-stick tape to
attach the letters.

Advent

Banner 7

48" × 63"

Wording is interchangeable as suggested in Advent Set 1–4.

Advent

Banner 8

48" × 48"

The pink candle is for Jubilate Sunday—the third Sunday of Advent.

WATCH
PEACE
GLORY
JESUS
BEHOLD

JOY
JESUS
GLORY
COME
WATCH

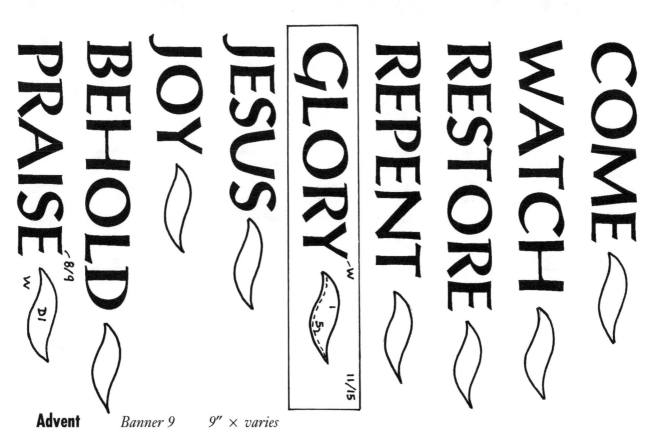

Advent   *Banner 9   9″ × varies*

Read "Bans That Accumulate Week by Week," page 22, as well as "Markers and Watercolor Paints," page 25.

Any choice of words may be used on individual bans. Allow a 3-inch margin at the base and a 5-inch margin at the top. Use a blue background with white letters and yellow flames or a white background with blue letters and yellow flames. Flames from Advent Banners 7 or 8 may be used instead.

Advent   *Banner 10   45″ × 72″*

The length of the banner will vary according to the height of the words used.

This banner is to be hung for the whole Advent season. Select words according to Series A, B, or C as indicated on Series Set 1–4.

Advent

Banners 11–14 (Advent Set)

18" × 75"

Read "Bans That Accumulate Week by Week," page 22, and "Bans Used as a Group," page 22.

This Advent ban set may be hung one Sunday at a time beginning with Banner 11. The bans symbolize God's plan of salvation through Jesus Christ—birth, ministry, death, and resurrection. Bans 13–14 may be used for the Lenten and Easter seasons. Use sequined or very shiny ribbon for the star. The candle base is blue with white design lines. Black lines are used for the flame and for the top curve line of the candle.

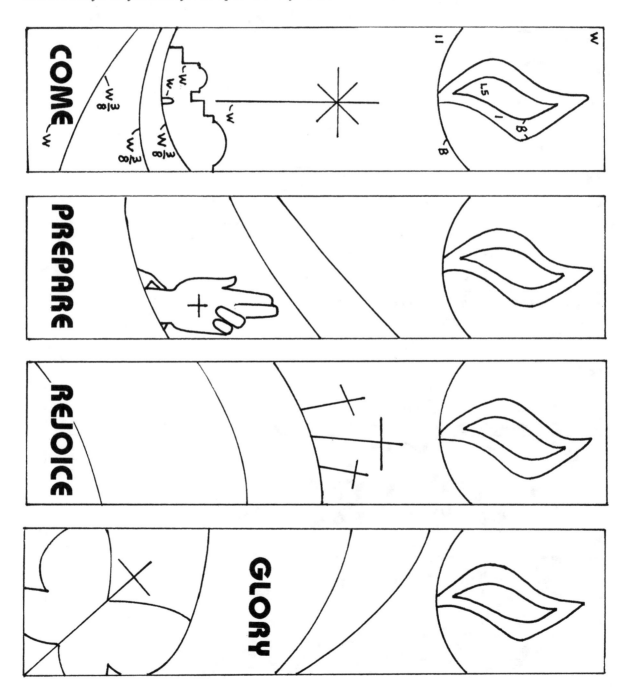

Advent/Christmas

Banner 15
48" × 60"

Display one flame and halo each week in Advent until all four flames are lighted for Christmas. Use double-stick tape.

Christmas

Banner 16A   Matthew 1:23

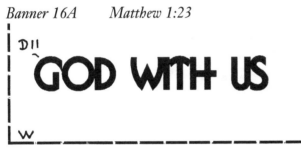

Christmas

Banner 16   39" × 78"   Luke 2:14

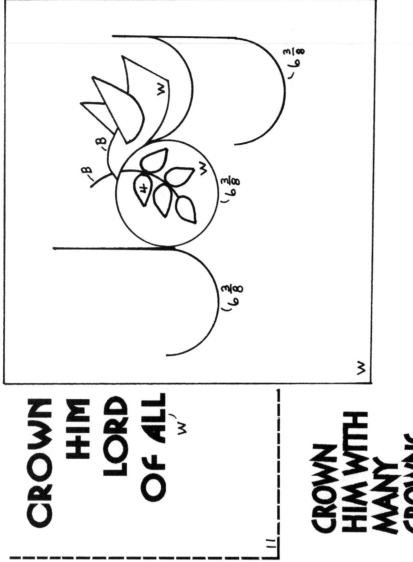

CROWN
HIM
LORD
OF ALL

CROWN
HIM WITH
MANY
CROWNS

Christmas

Banner 17
48" × 48"

Christmas

Banner 18
45" × 78"
Luke 2:14

Christmas

Banner 18A
Words are taken from the hymn "All Hail the Power of Jesus' Name."

Christmas

Banner 18B
Also useful for Easter and for general times of the year.
Words are taken from the hymn "Crown Him with Many Crowns."

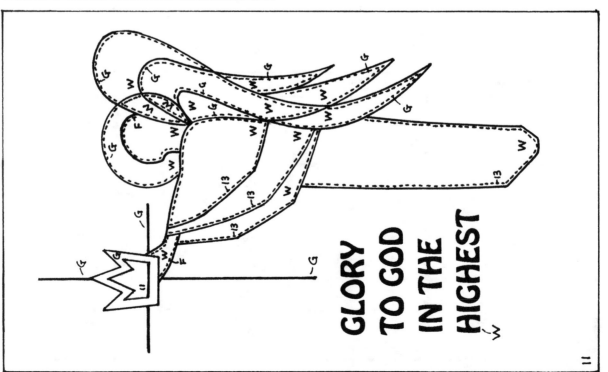

GLORY
TO GOD
IN THE
HIGHEST

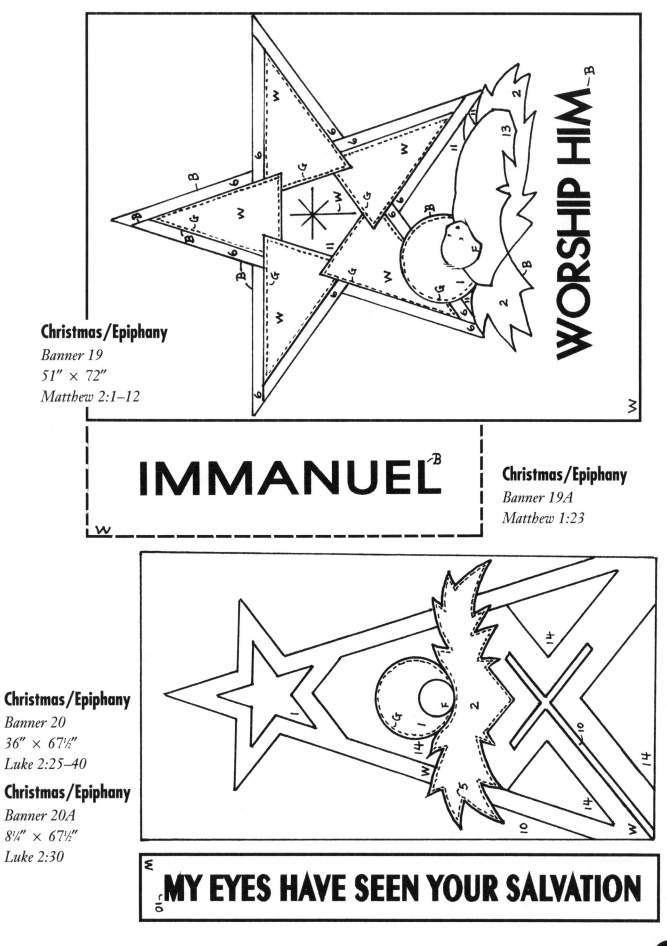

Christmas/Epiphany

Banner 19
51" × 72"
Matthew 2:1–12

WORSHIP HIM

IMMANUEL

Christmas/Epiphany

Banner 19A
Matthew 1:23

Christmas/Epiphany

Banner 20
36" × 67½"
Luke 2:25–40

Christmas/Epiphany

Banner 20A
8¼" × 67½"
Luke 2:30

MY EYES HAVE SEEN YOUR SALVATION

Christmas/Epiphany

Banner 21
40½" × 58"
Second Sunday after the Epiphany
John 1:14

Christmas/Epiphany /Good Shepherd Sunday

Banner 22
48" × 84"
Micah 5:2–4; Matthew 2:6

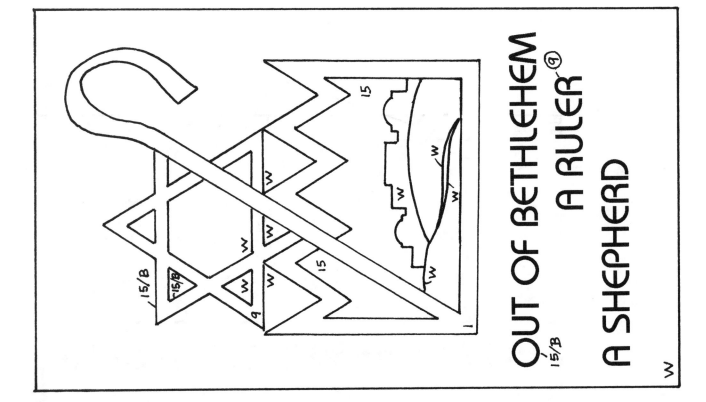

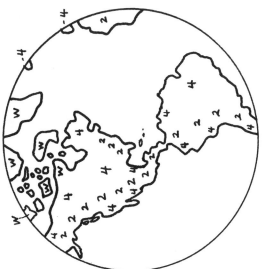

Christmas/Epiphany

Banner 23   42″ × 72″   Luke 2:14; 19:38

Banner 23A
Use watercolor paints to color the globe.
Read "Markers and Watercolor Paints," page 25.

Epiphany Sunday

Banner 24   36″ × 70″   Matthew 2:1–12
Read "Sequins and Gold Trim," page 21.

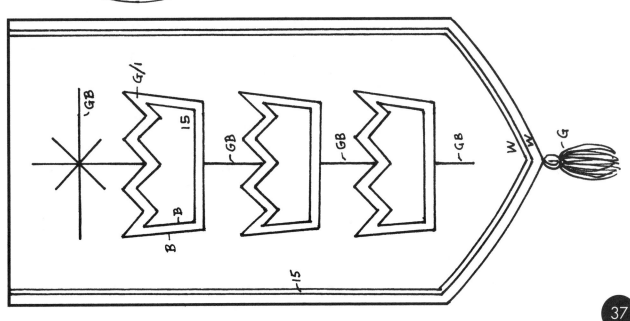

REPENT ✝

15

Ash Wednesday

Banner 25   9″ × 36″

Smear ashes to form the cross shape.

HOSANNA *10 W*

Palm Sunday

Banner 26

9″ × 72″

HOSANNA *W 15*

Palm Sunday

Banner 27

9″ × 72″

IN THE HIGHEST

HOSANNA

HOSANNA

HOSANNA

HOSANNA

Palm Sunday

Banner 28   45″ × 84″

Matthew 21:9, 15

Passion Week Series

Banners 29–33   39″ × 54″

This portion of the design in the detail is glued to the background. The rest of the design changes with double-stick tape. Read "Double-Stick Tape and Post-It Brand Glue Stick," page 23.

Palm Sunday   Banner 29   Matthew 21:9, 15

GIVEN FOR YOU +G 15/17

Maundy Thursday /Communion

Banner 30   *Luke 22:19*

IT IS + + + G **FINISHED** 15/17

Good Friday

Banner 31   *John 19:30*

CHRIST HAS RISEN 15/17

Easter

Banner 32   *Matthew 28:6*

JESUS + SHALL + REIGN + 15/17

Easter/Missions

Banner 33   *Words are taken from the hymn "Jesus Shall Reign"*

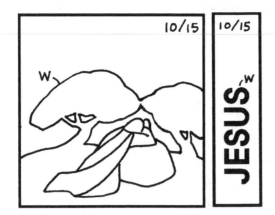

JESUS'ʷ

10/15

10/15

JUDAS

HEROD

PETER

Lent

Banners 34–67
24″ × 24″
ban 6″ × 24″
Banners and bans may be used individually or by groups to fit any series of sermons for Lent.

Lent/People of Passion Week

Banners 34–43

CAIAPHAS

PILATE

BARABBAS

SIMON OF CYRENE

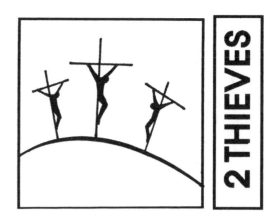

2 THIEVES

MARY

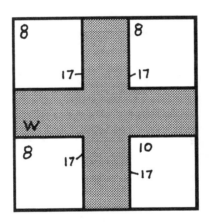

DISCIPLE

Lent / Events

Banners 44–47

Ash Wednesday

Banner 44

The cross is white with ashes smeared in that area.

Palm Sunday

Banner 45

Maundy Thursday / Communion

Banner 46

Good Friday

Banner 47

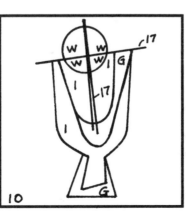

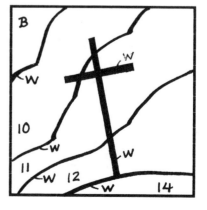

41

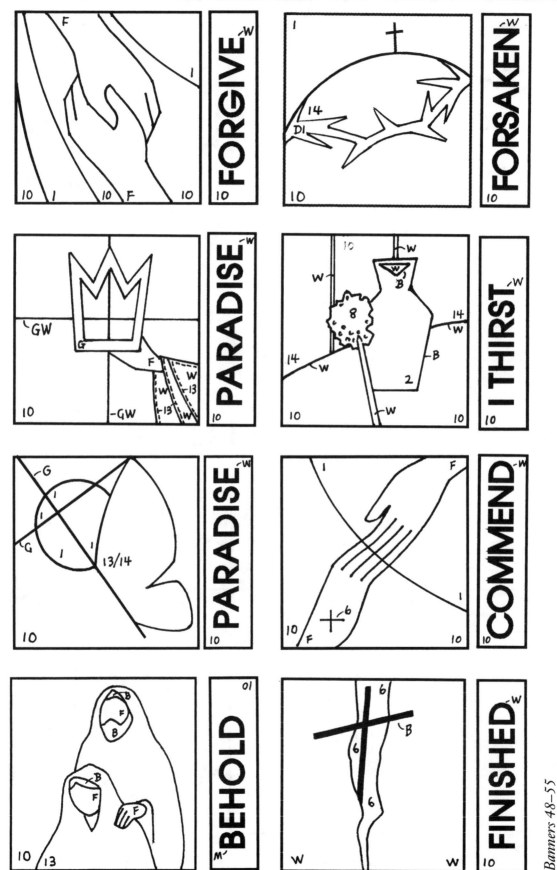

Banners 48–55

Use the colors indicated or have all the backgrounds purple with white felt-strip lines and white letters. Read "Directions for Applying Felt Strips," page 18.

Use either 49 or 50 for Paradise.

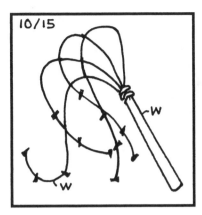

Banner 56 whip

Banner 59 sign posted on the cross

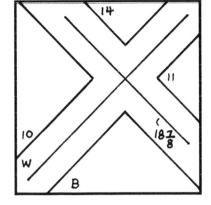

Banner 57 crown of thorns

Banner 60 Christ's garments

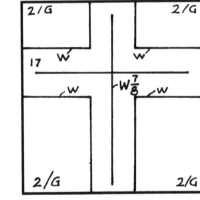

Banners 63–64

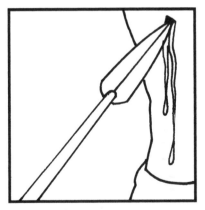

Banner 58 spear

Banner 61 nails

Banner 62 cross and nails

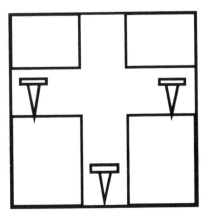

Lent/Maundy Thursday/Communion

Banner 65

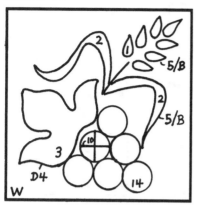

Lent/Good Friday

Banners 66, 67

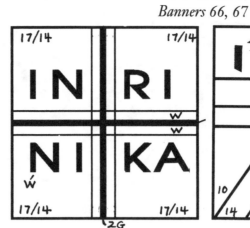

Use a purple background with white lines and letters.
Interfaced velour makes a rich purple background.

Good Friday/Lent

Banner 68   36″ × 60″   Isaiah 53:4

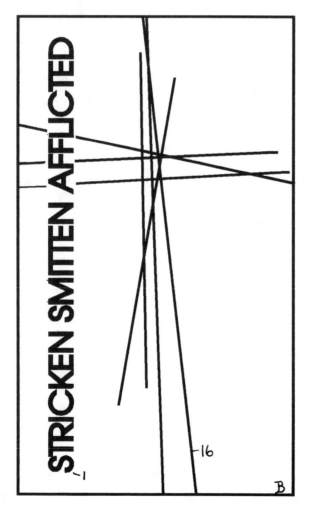

Good Friday/Lent

Banner 69   39″ × 61″

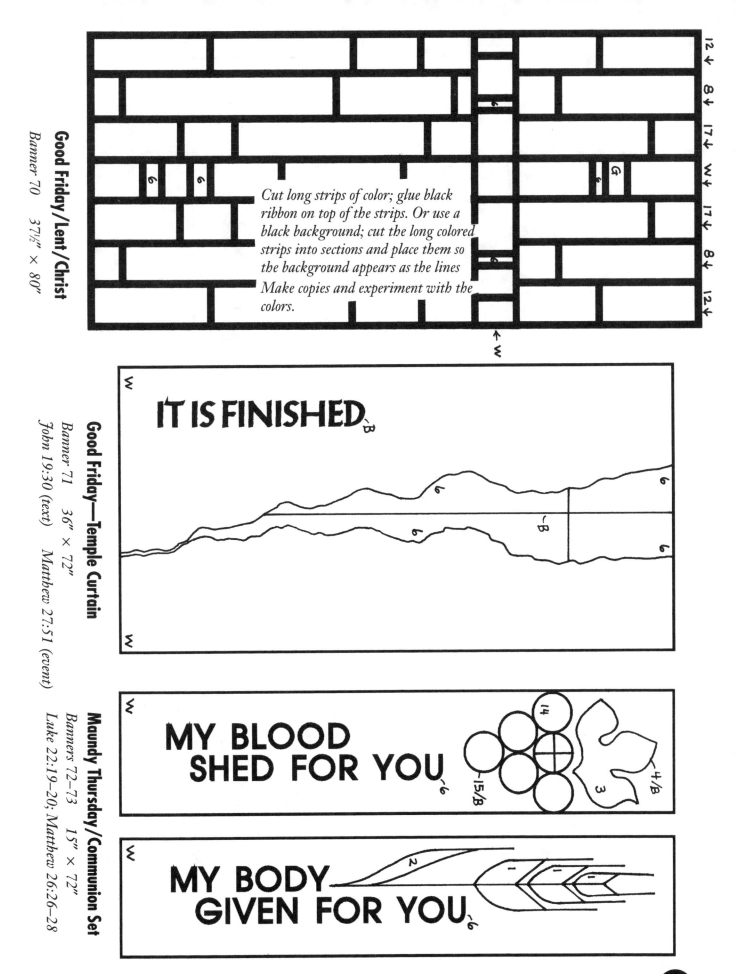

Good Friday/Lent/Christ

Banner 70   37½" × 80"

Cut long strips of color; glue black ribbon on top of the strips. Or use a black background; cut the long colored strips into sections and place them so the background appears as the lines Make copies and experiment with the colors.

Good Friday—Temple Curtain

Banner 71   36" × 72"
John 19:30 (text)   Matthew 27:51 (event)

IT IS FINISHED

Maundy Thursday/Communion Set

Banners 72–73   15" × 72"
Luke 22:19–20; Matthew 26:26–28

MY BLOOD SHED FOR YOU

MY BODY GIVEN FOR YOU

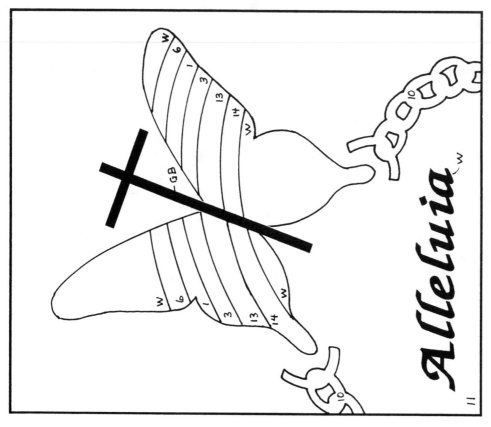

Easter/Funeral

Banner 74

48" × 58"

Read "Directions for Painting a Watercolor Rainbow," page 26, and "Bans Extend the Life of a Banner," page 22.

Easter/Funeral

Banner 75

43" × 63"

Read "Markers and Watercolor Paints," page 25.

Easter/Funeral

Banner 75A

Matthew 28:6

Easter/Funeral

Banner 76

15" × 78"   *Words are taken from the hymn "Jesus Lives! The Victory's Won"*   *1 Corinthians 15:55, 57*

THE VICTORY'S WON

Easter/Funeral

Banner 77

15" × 72"

Job 19:25

I KNOW THAT MY REDEEMER LIVES

Easter/Funeral

Banner 78

45" × 60"

Job 19:25

Symbolism:

3 circles=Trinity

palm leaves=praise to the King

flames=faith in resurrection

Alpha, Omega=first and last, eternity

Easter/Funeral

Banner 79   *15" × 72"*   *Matthew 28:6*

he has risen

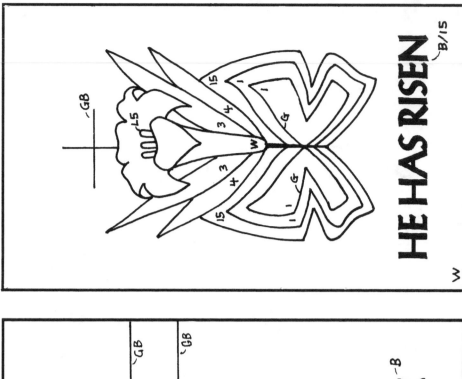

HE HAS RISEN

Easter/Funeral
Banner 80
36″ × 60″
Matthew 28:6;
Mark 16:6; Luke
24:6

Easter/Funeral
Banner 81
36″ × 60″
John 20:29
Banner 81A
Job 19:25

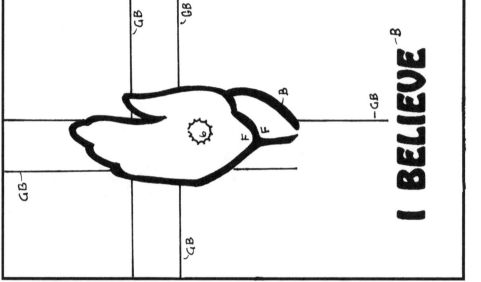

I BELIEVE

MY REDEEMER LIVES

Alleluia

Easter/Funeral
Banner 82
36″ × 60″
The circle may be
colored as a globe
with watercolor
paint (see Banner
23A). Read
"Markers and
Watercolor
Paints," page 25.

Transfiguration

Banner 83
42" × 72"
Luke 9:35

Ascension/Confirmation/ Blessing

Banner 84
39" × 64"
Matthew 28:20 Confirmation

Banner 84A
Numbers 6:24 Blessing

++THE LORD BLESS AND KEEP YOU++⁶

Banner 84B
John 14:27 Confirmation

MY PEACE

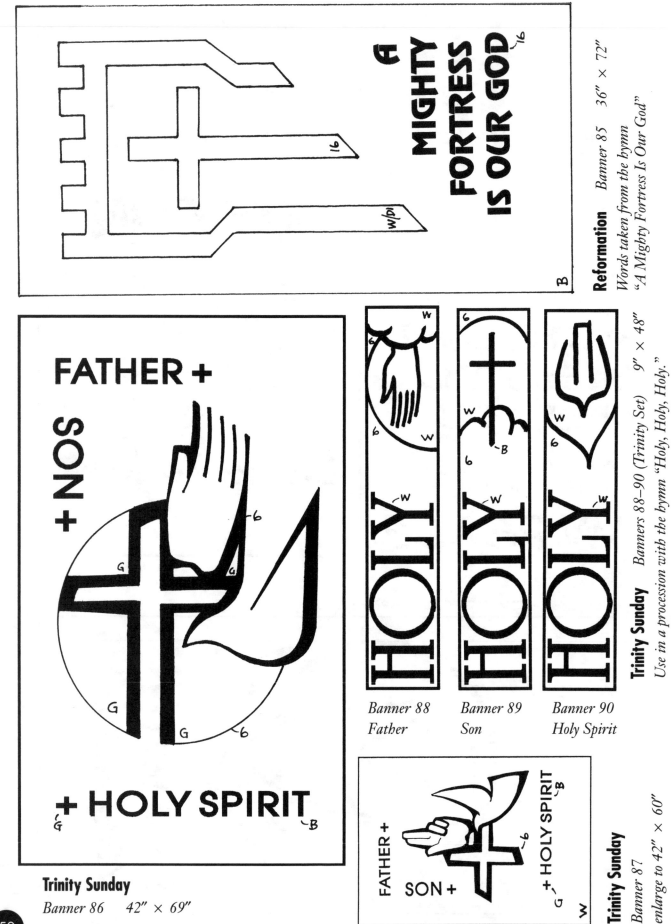

Reformation *Banner 85   36″ × 72″*

Words taken from the hymn
"A Mighty Fortress Is Our God"

Trinity Sunday   *Banners 88–90 (Trinity Set)   9″ × 48″*
Use in a procession with the hymn "Holy, Holy, Holy."

Banner 88   *Banner 89*   *Banner 90*
Father   *Son*   *Holy Spirit*

Trinity Sunday
Banner 86   42″ × 69″

Trinity Sunday
Banner 87
enlarge to 42″ × 60″

Trinity Sunday

Banner 91
46" × 60"
Use 5 mm sequins.
Read "Sequins and Gold Trim," page 21.

HOLY + HOLY + HOLY

FATHER   SON

HOLY SPIRIT

ALL GLORY AND HONOR

Banner 91B optional ban   7" × 60"
Words are taken from the hymn "Holy, Holy, Holy."

Banner 91A optional ban   7" × 60"

Trinity Sunday

Banners 93–95 (Trinity Set)
24" × 24"

Banner 93   Father

Banner 94   Son

Banner 95   Holy Spirit

HOLY
HOLY
HOLY

Trinity Sunday

Banner 92—set of three bans
9" × 48"
Use in a procession with the hymn "Holy, Holy, Holy."

51

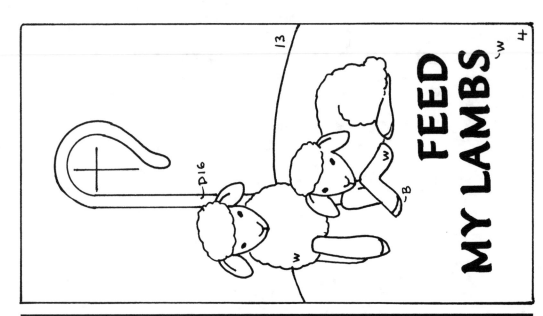

FEED MY LAMBS

MY SHEEP LISTEN TO MY VOICE

Good Shepherd Sunday

Banner 96
35" × 66"
John 21:15
Make a side ban for the hymn "I Am Jesus' Little Lamb."

Confirmation

Banner 96A
7½" × 66"
John 10:27

Good Shepherd Sunday/Ordination *Banner 97   15" × 72"   John 21:17*

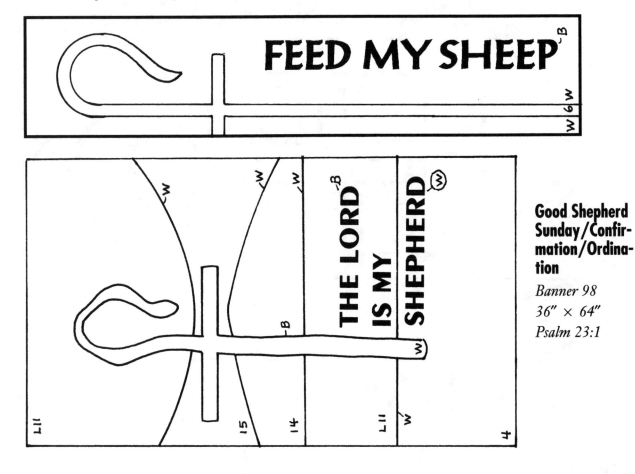

FEED MY SHEEP

THE LORD IS MY SHEPHERD

Good Shepherd Sunday/Confirmation/Ordination

Banner 98
36" × 64"
Psalm 23:1

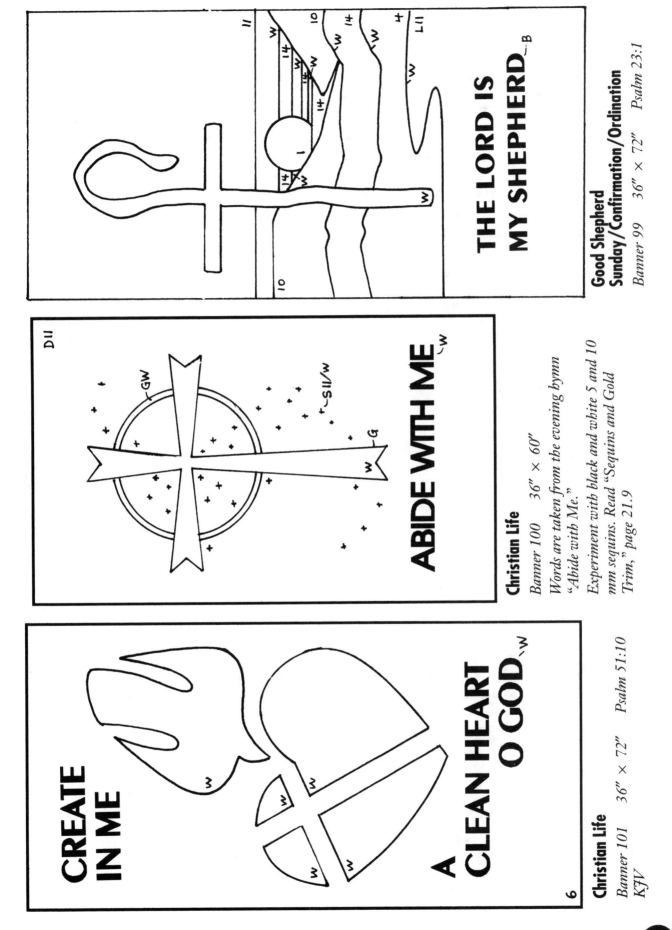

THE LORD IS MY SHEPHERD —B

Good Shepherd
Sunday/Confirmation/Ordination
Banner 99   36" × 72"   Psalm 23:1

ABIDE WITH ME —w

Christian Life

Banner 100   36" × 60"
Words are taken from the evening hymn
"Abide with Me."

Experiment with black and white 5 and 10
mm sequins. Read "Sequins and Gold
Trim," page 21.9

CREATE IN ME

A CLEAN HEART O GOD —w

Christian Life
Banner 101   36" × 72"   Psalm 51:10
KJV

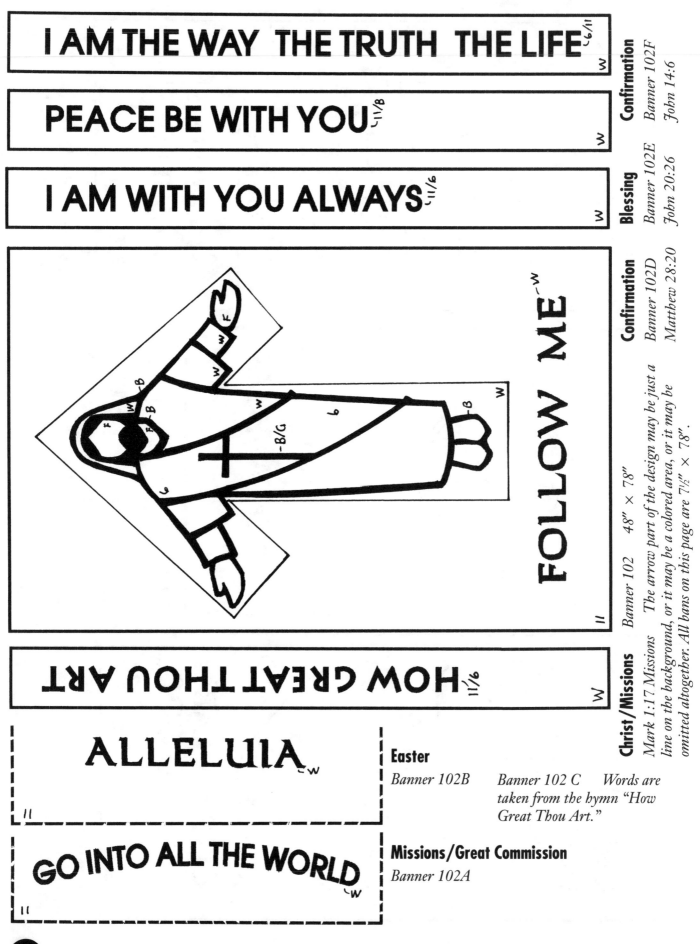

I AM THE WAY THE TRUTH THE LIFE

11/9 W

Confirmation Banner 102F John 14:6

PEACE BE WITH YOU

11/8 W

Confirmation Banner 102E John 20:26

I AM WITH YOU ALWAYS

11/9 W

Blessing Banner 102D Matthew 28:20

FOLLOW ME

11 W

Christ / Missions Banner 102 48" × 78"

Mark 1:17 Missions

The arrow part of the design may be just a line on the background, or it may be a colored area, or it may be omitted altogether. All bans on this page are 7½" × 78".

HOW GREAT THOU ART

11/9 W

Confirmation

ALLELUIA

W

Easter Banner 102B

Banner 102 C   Words are taken from the hymn "How Great Thou Art."

GO INTO ALL THE WORLD

W

Missions/Great Commission Banner 102A

PROCLAIM
HIS KINGDOM

Christ/Mission
Banner 103
36″ × 60″

Christ/Funeral
Banner 103A
James 1:12

Confirmation
Banner 103B
Revelation 2:10

RECEIVE
THE CROWN
+ + + OF LIFE
BE FAITHFUL

Christ/Confirmation
Banner 104   30″ × 48″

GROW +
IN GOD'S
GRACE + + +

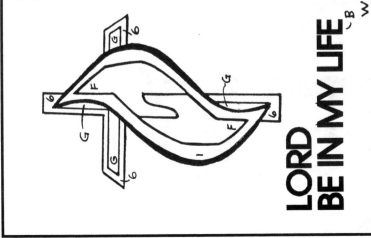

LORD
BE IN MY LIFE

Christ/Confirmation
Banner 105   30″ × 48″

Christ

Banner 106
45″ × 48″
Revelation 1:8; 21:6; 22:13

Christ/Confirmation

Banner 107
30″ × 48″

Christ/Missions/Confirmation

Banner 108   41″ × 64½″
John 8:12

The circle may be colored as a globe with watercolor paints (see Banner 23A). Read "Markers and Watercolor Paints," page 25.

Christ/Confirmation

Banner 109
27" × 54"
John 8:12

Christ

Banner 110
33" × 45"
Exchange wording for the hymn title "Jesus, Savior, Pilot Me."
Read "Double-Stick Tape and Post-It Brand Glue Stick," page 23.

Christ

Banner 111
33" × 39"

Symbol Designs

Banners 112–116
These symbol designs are usable for bans and banners. Use an overhead projector to enlarge or reduce the size of the designs.
112 symbol for ICHTHUS (Jesus Christ, Son of God, Savior)
112–116 symbols for CHI RHO (first two letters in Christ)
113 CHI RHO

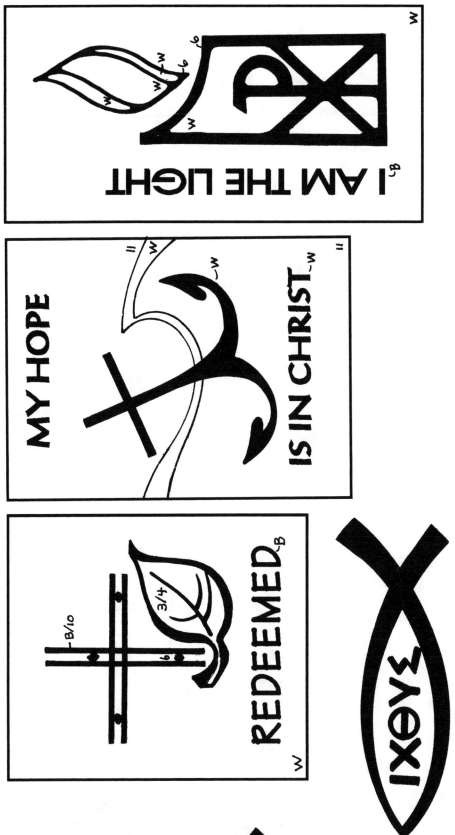

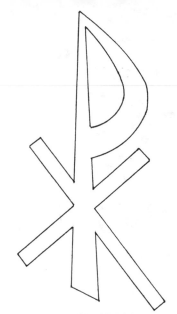

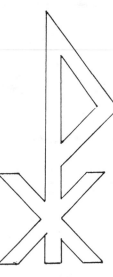

114 CHI RHO *115 CHI RHO* *116 CHI RHO* *117 CHI RHO*

Christ

Banner 118   33″ × 45″

Christ/Christian Life/Confirmation

Banner 119   30″ × 48″
Philippians 1:21

Christ/Confirmation

Banner 120   36″ × 48″
John 15:5

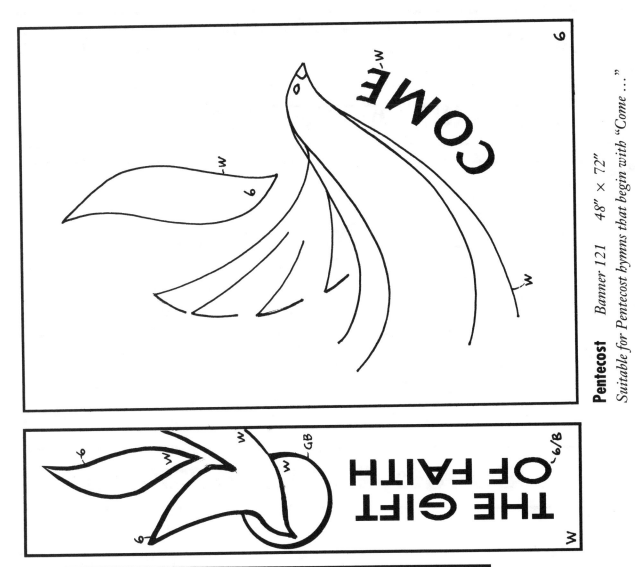

Pentecost *Banner 121 48" × 72"*

Suitable for Pentecost hymns that begin with "Come …"

Pentecost/Baptism

Banner 122
15" × 72"
Reference to Ephesians 2:8–9

Pentecost/ Christian Life

Banner 123
45" × 60"
Galatians 5:25

FAITH + THE GIFT OF THE HOLY SPIRIT

THE FRUIT OF THE SPIRIT

Pentecost

Banner 124   36" × 81"

Use the banner alone or with any of the three optional bans.

REJOICE IN GOD'S GRACE

124C
7½" × 81"

Pentecost

Banners 125–133 Fruit of the Spirit set 13½" × 63" or 15" × 63"

These bans may be used individually, as set of nine, or in combination with Banner 124. Read "Bans Used as a Group," page 22, and "Bans Used in Addition to a Banner," page 21.

125 Love

LOVE

126 Peace

PEACE

127 Joy

JOY

128 Self-control

SELF-CONTROL

129 Faithfulness

FAITHFULNESS

130 Gentleness

GENTLENESS

131 Goodness

GOODNESS

132 Kindness

KINDNESS

133 Patience

PATIENCE

Pentecost

Banner 134   36" × 66"

134A optional ban

Words are taken from the hymn "Holy Spirit, Light Divine."

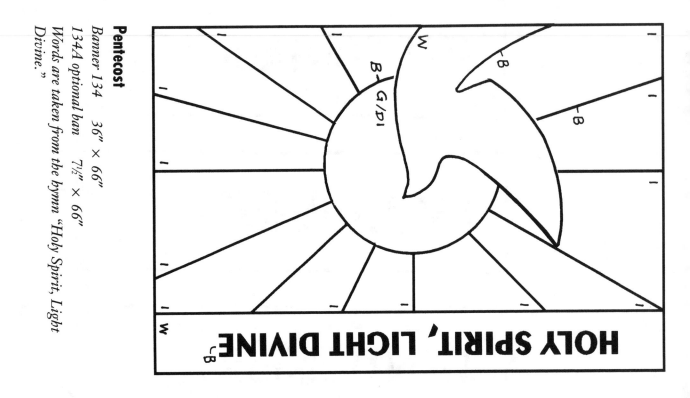

HOLY SPIRIT, LIGHT DIVINE

Pentecost/Praise   *Banner 135   19½" × 72"*

REJOICE

Pentecost   *Banner 136   36" × 72"*

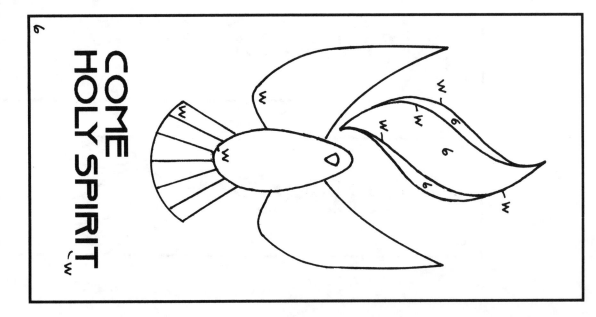

COME HOLY SPIRIT

W

Pentecost/Confirmation/Christian Life

Banner 137   36" × 72"   Galatians 5:25

LIVE BY
THE SPIRIT

GROW
IN GOD'S
GRACE
L B

Confirmation   *Banner 137B*

BY GRACE
YOU ARE SAVED
L B

Christian Life   *Banner 137A*

Pentecost

Banner 138
9" × 48"

Ephesians 2:8

COME

Pentecost/Christian Life

Banner 139   46½" × 73"

W

HOPE + LOVE + LIFE

FAITH + H
GB
GB

W

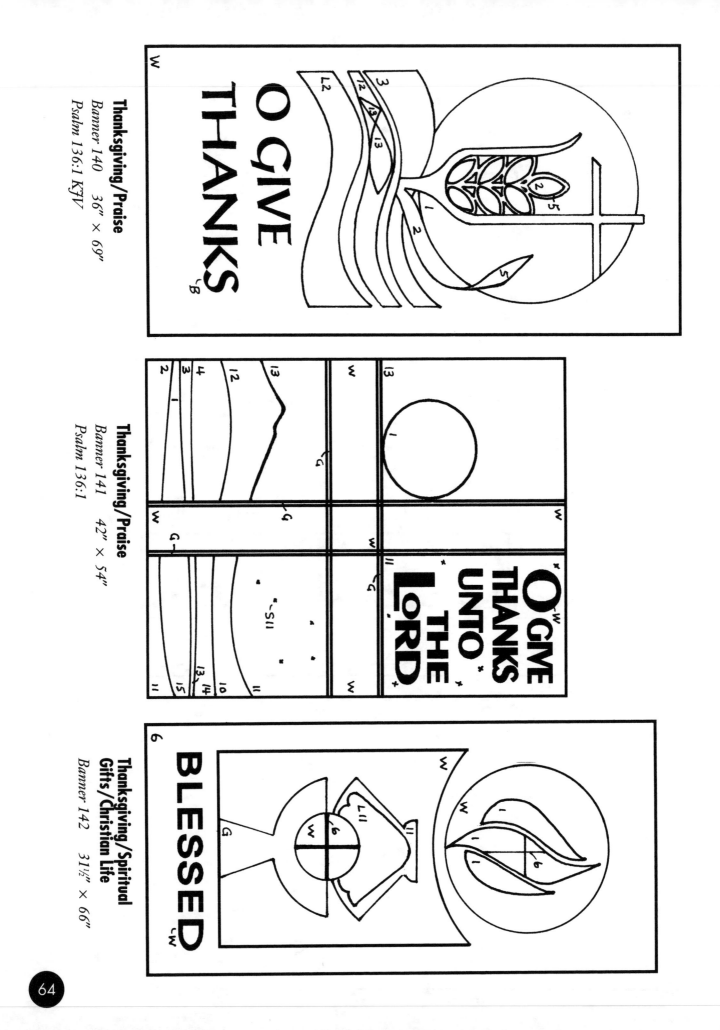

Thanksgiving/Praise
Banner 140   36" × 69"
Psalm 136:1 KJV

O GIVE
THANKS

Thanksgiving/Praise
Banner 141   42" × 54"
Psalm 136:1

O GIVE
THANKS
UNTO
THE
LORD

**Thanksgiving/Spiritual
Gifts/Christian Life**
Banner 142   31½" × 66"

BLESSED

Thanksgiving/Prayer   *Banner 143A*   *Psalm 136:1 KJV*   **Prayer**   *Banner 143*   *33″ × 60″*

Prayer
Banner 144   *9″ × 48″*

Prayer   *Banner 145*   *15″ × 78¾″*   *Psalm 141:2*

Prayer
Banner 146
9″ × 48″

Prayer/Confirmation
Banner 147A
12″ × 57″
Psalm 55:22

Prayer/Confirmation
Banner 147
21″ × 68¼″

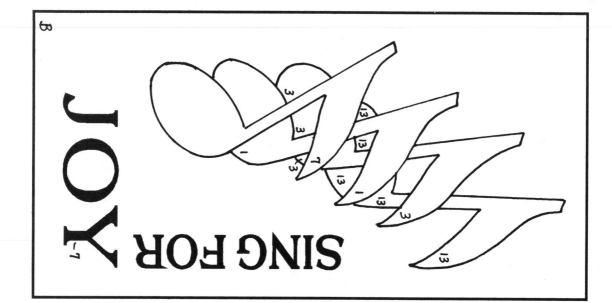

Praise

Banner 148
36" × 72"
Psalm 5:11; 67:4; 81:1;
92:4; 95:1; 96:12

Praise

Banner 149
51" × 46½"
Psalm 96:1

Praise

Banner 150
9" × 72"

Baptism

Banner 151
42″ × 60″
Reference to Isaiah 43:1

Baptism

Banner 152
15″ × 76″
Use the baptismal candidate's name.

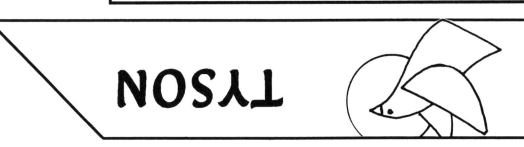

Baptism

Banner 153
30″ × 54″
Romans 6:3–4
May use with or without the side bans.

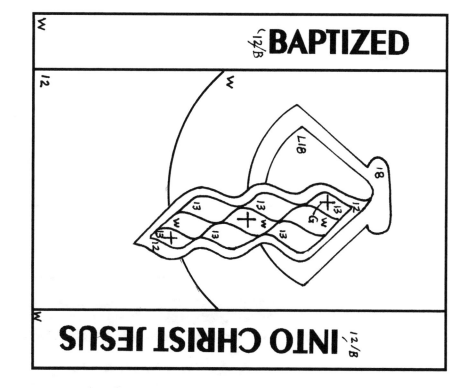

Baptism

Banner 154
39" × 60"
John 15:9

Baptism

Banner 155
45" × 75"
Reference to Ephesians 2:8–9

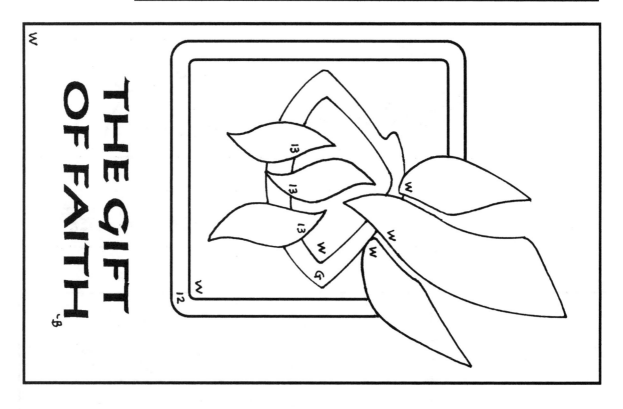

Baptism   *Banner 156   18" × 66"   Use the baptismal candidate's name.*

Glue the three ribbons on the shell portion and let the rest of the ribbon hang loose from the banner. Read "Sequins and Gold Trim," page 21.

Baptism

Banner 157

40½″ × 48″

The name may be changed with each Baptism. Read "Double-Stick Tape and Post-It Brand Glue Stick," page 23.

Baptism

Banner 158

52″ × 67½″

John 3:5

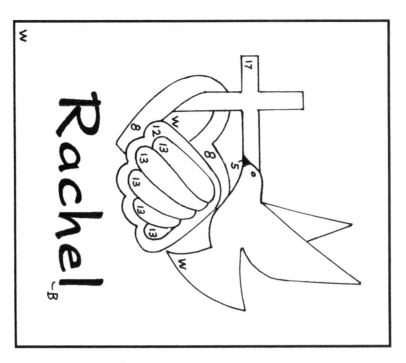

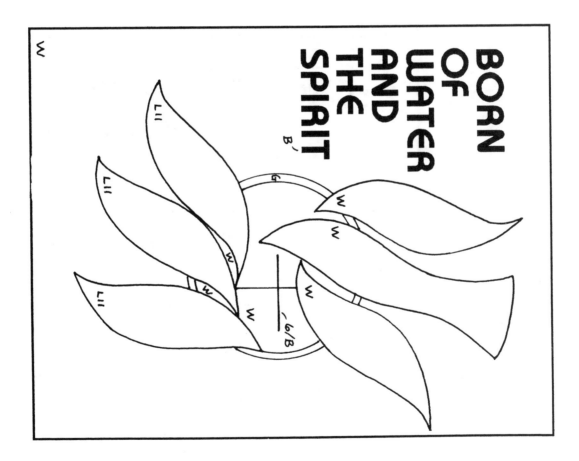

Baptism

Banner 159
37" × 57"

159A optional ban
12" × 57"
Acts 22:16

159B–C may be used together with Banner 159. Mark 16:16
11" × 57"

159C
7½" × 57"

Baptism

Banner 160
31" × 45"

The three crosses symbolize being baptized in the name of the Father and of the Son and of the Holy Spirit.

The name may be changed with each Baptism. Read "Double-Stick Tape and Post-It Brand Glue Stick," page 23.

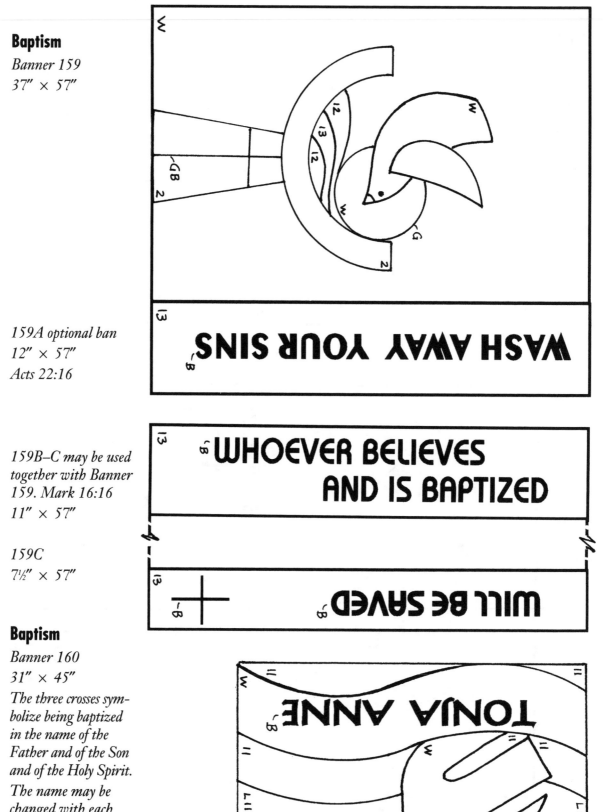

God's Word

Banner 161
52½" × 66"
Colossians 3:16

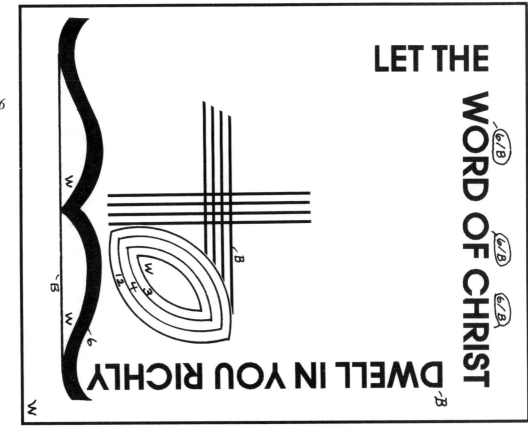

God's Word

Banner 162
37" × 46½"
Romans 10:17
KJV

God's Word
Banner 163
42" × 51"
John 17:17

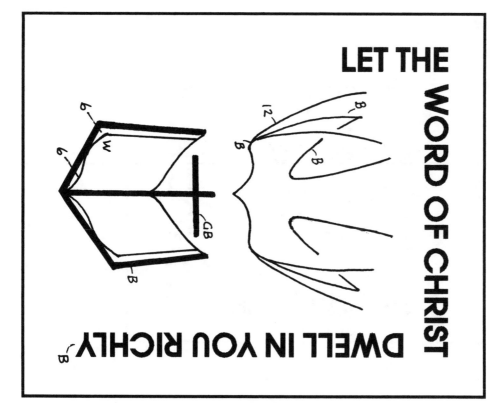

God's Word
Banner 164
48" × 62"
Colossians 3:16

Gods' Word

Banner 165
51" × 56¼"
2 Peter 1:19

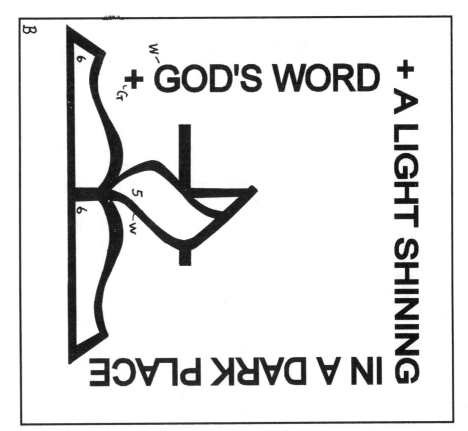

God's Word

Banner 166
40½" × 60"
Psalm 119:11

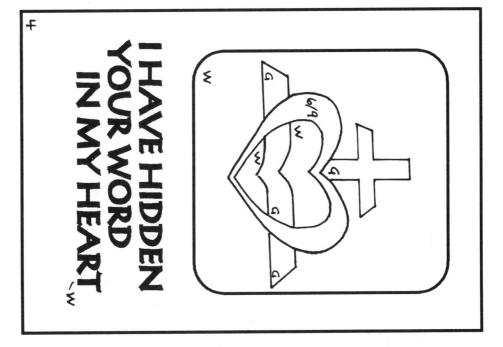

YOUR WORD IS A LAMP TO MY FEET

God's Word *Banner 167* *15″ × 78″* *Psalm 119:105*

God's Word *Banner 168* *45″ × 60″* *Psalm 119:74*

MY WORD WILL NEVER PASS AWAY

I PUT MY HOPE IN YOUR WORD

God's Word/Confirmation

Banner 169A *Matthew 24:35*

God's Word *Banner 169* *45″ × 78″* *Psalm 119:89*

YOUR WORD O LORD IS ETERNAL

God's Word

Banner 170
42" × 54"
Ephesians 6:17

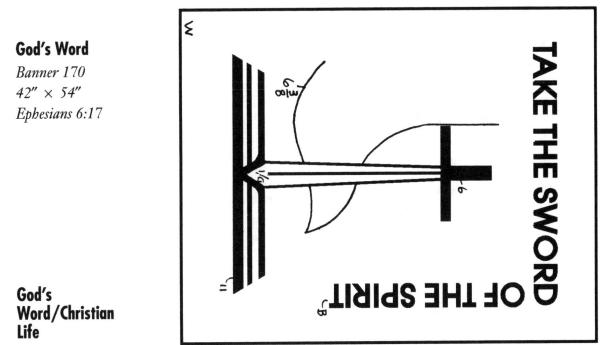

God's Word/Christian Life

Banner 171
15" × 78"
Psalm 25:4

God's Word

Banner 172
42" × 54"
Words are taken from the hymn "Thy Strong Word."

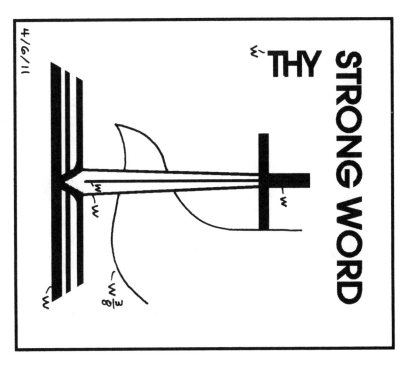

Missions

Banner 173
55½″ × 61½″
Words are taken from the hymn "Go Tell It on the Mountain."

Missions

Banner 174
9″ × 72″
Matthew 4:19

Missions

Banner 175
42″ × 60″
Words are taken from the hymn "This Little Gospel Light of Mine."

SALVATION
FOR ALL ~w

WE ARE CHRIST'S AMBASSADORS

Missions *Banner 176   57" × 84"*
This may be reduced in size. Make sure the letters are at least 3 inches in height.

HERE I AM
SEND ME ~10/B

THE HARVEST
IS WAITING

Confirmation
*Banner 176A
2 Corinthians
5:20*

Missions
*Banner 177
45" × 72"
Words are taken
from the hymn
"Hark, the
Voice of Jesus
Calling."*

Missions

Banner 178
39" × 48"
Matthew 4:19

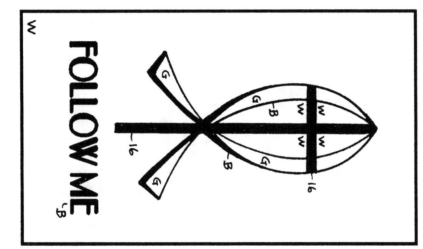

Missions

Banner 179
30" × 52"
Mark 1:17

Missions

Banner 180
36" × 45"
Mark 1:17

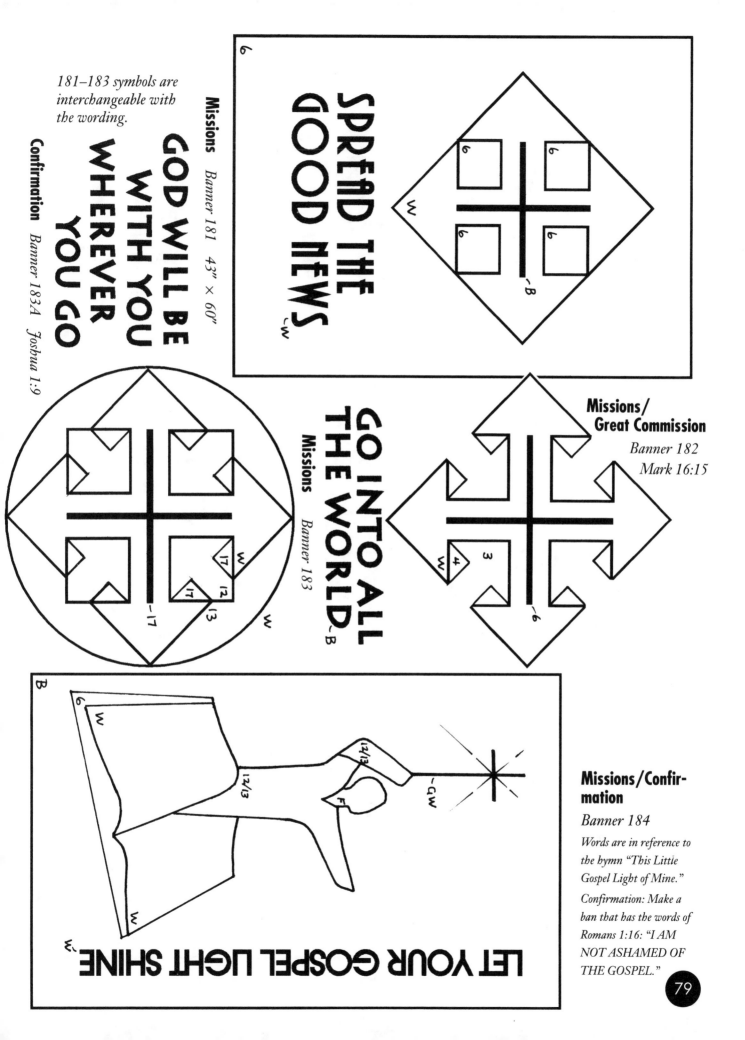

181–183 symbols are interchangeable with the wording.

Missions *Banner 181 43" × 60"*

SPREAD THE GOOD NEWS

Missions/Great Commission
Banner 182
Mark 16:15

Missions
Banner 183

GO INTO ALL THE WORLD

GOD WILL BE WITH YOU WHEREVER YOU GO

Confirmation *Banner 183A Joshua 1:9*

Missions/Confirmation

Banner 184

Words are in reference to the hymn "This Little Gospel Light of Mine."

Confirmation: Make a ban that has the words of Romans 1:16: "I AM NOT ASHAMED OF THE GOSPEL."

LET YOUR GOSPEL LIGHT SHINE

Missions

Banner 185   34" × 66"

*185A–185B optional bans
The bans may be used
together or individually
with Banner 185.
Cut the bottoms of
the bans to match
the angle of the
banner. The
wording for
Ban 185A is
from the hymn
"Lift High the
Cross."*

Missions

*Banner 186
15" × 67½"
Use 5 mm iri-
descent sequins.
Read "Sequins
and Gold
Trim," page
21.*

Missions

*Banner 187
36" × 66"
Make copies of
the design and
experiment with
colors.*

LIFT HIGH THE CROSS

PROCLAIM CHRIST

MY GOSPEL LIGHT

INTO ALL THE WORLD

Missions

Banner 188
45" × 51"
Mark 1:14–20

Missions

Banner 189
9" × 72"
Mark 1:17

Missions

Banner 190
48" × 72"

Words are taken from the hymn "Go Tell It on the Mountain."

Christmas

Banner 190A

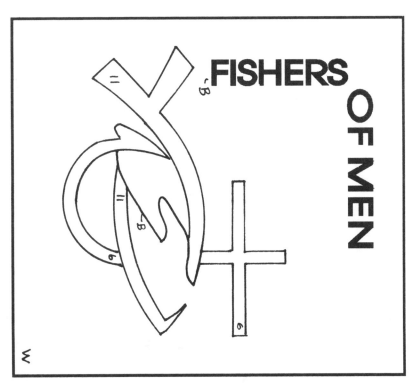

Ordination/Installation
Banner 191
48″ × 66″

Ordination/Installation
Banner 192
38″ × 66″

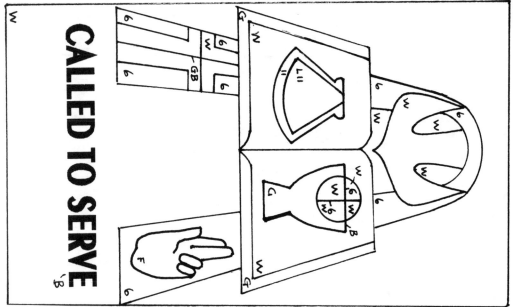

Wedding/ Anniversary

Banners 193–201 These banners may have side bans with the names of the couple.

Wedding/ Anniversary

Banner 193 39" × 58"

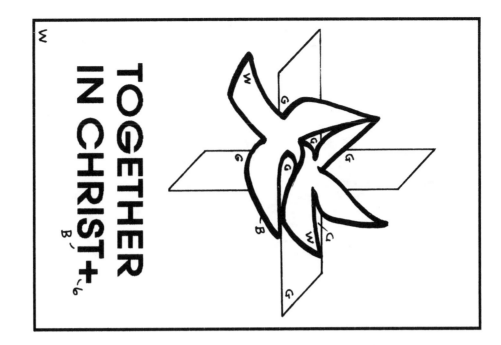

Wedding/ Anniversary

Banner 194 36" × 60" Colossians 2:2 You may also use the words to the hymn title "Blest Be the Tie That Binds." Increase the banner's length or use a side ban for the new wording.

Wedding/ Anniversary

Banner 195 33" × 54" 1 John 4:7

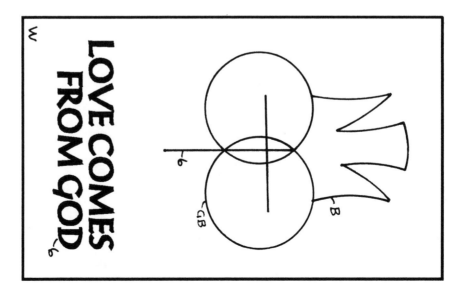

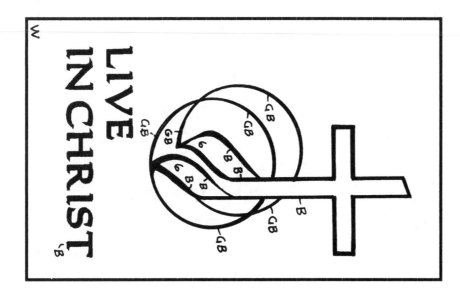

Wedding/Anniversary

Banner 196
33" × 54"

Wedding/Anniversary

Banner 197
33" × 48"
*For the cross read
"Sequins and Gold
Trim," page 21.*

Wedding/Anniversary

Banner 198
36" × 48"

Wedding/Anniversary

Banner 199
32" × 53"

Wedding/Anniversary

Banner 200
48" × 60"
Ephesians 5:2

Wedding/Anniversary

Banner 200A

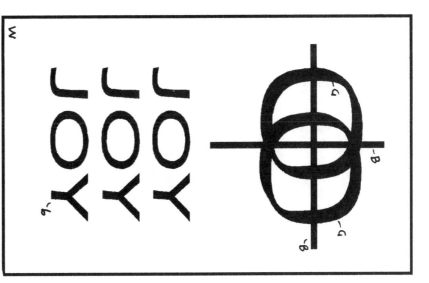

Wedding/Anniversary

Banner 201
37½" × 48"

Wedding/Christian Life

Banner 202
36" × 54"
Ephesians 5:2

Christian Life

Banner 203
36" × 66"
Reference to 1 Corinthians 13:13

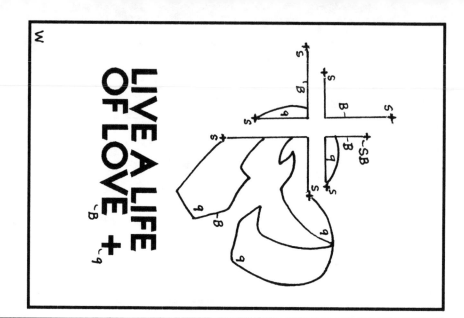

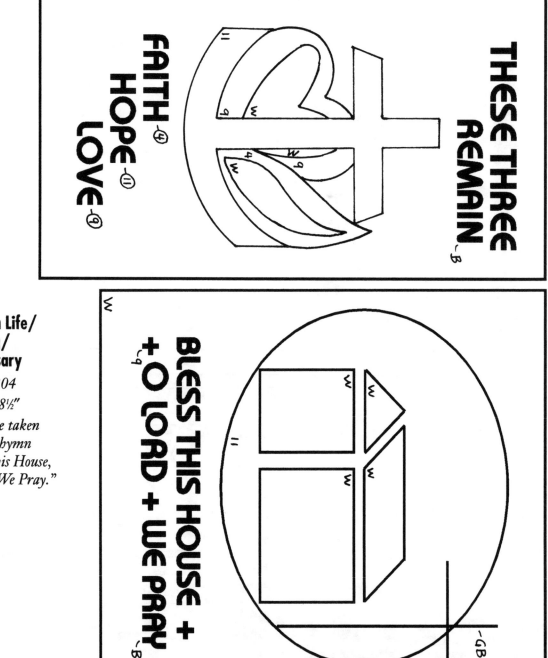

**Christian Life/
Wedding/
Anniversary**

Banner 204
51" × 58½"
*Words are taken
from the hymn
"Bless This House,
O Lord, We Pray."*

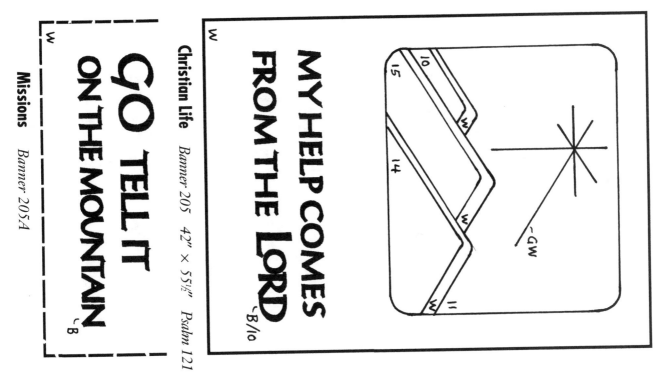

Missions *Banner 205A*

GO TELL IT ON THE MOUNTAIN

Christian Life *Banner 205* *42" × 55½"* *Psalm 121*

MY HELP COMES FROM THE LORD

Thanksgiving *Banner 206A* *Psalm 136:1*
Use light and dark green, orange, and white arrows.

O GIVE THANKS COME UNTO ME

JESUS CHRIST IS BORN

Christmas *Banner 205B*

Christian Life *Banner 206B* *Matthew 11:28 KJV*
Use varying shades of blues and/or purples for the arrows.

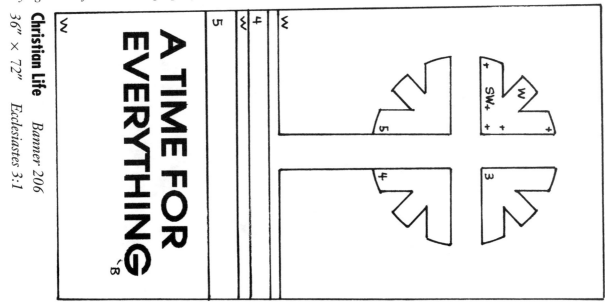

Christian Life *36" × 72"* *Banner 206* *Ecclesiastes 3:1*

A TIME FOR EVERYTHING

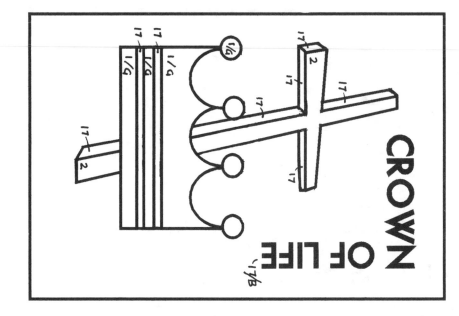

**Christian Life/
Confirmation**

Banner 207
36" × 54"
Revelation 2:10
207A–207B optional
bans
9" × 54"
Reference to Revela-
tion 2:10
These may be used
individually or
together with Banner
210 without words.

**Christian Life/
Christmas**

Banner 208
46" × 53½"

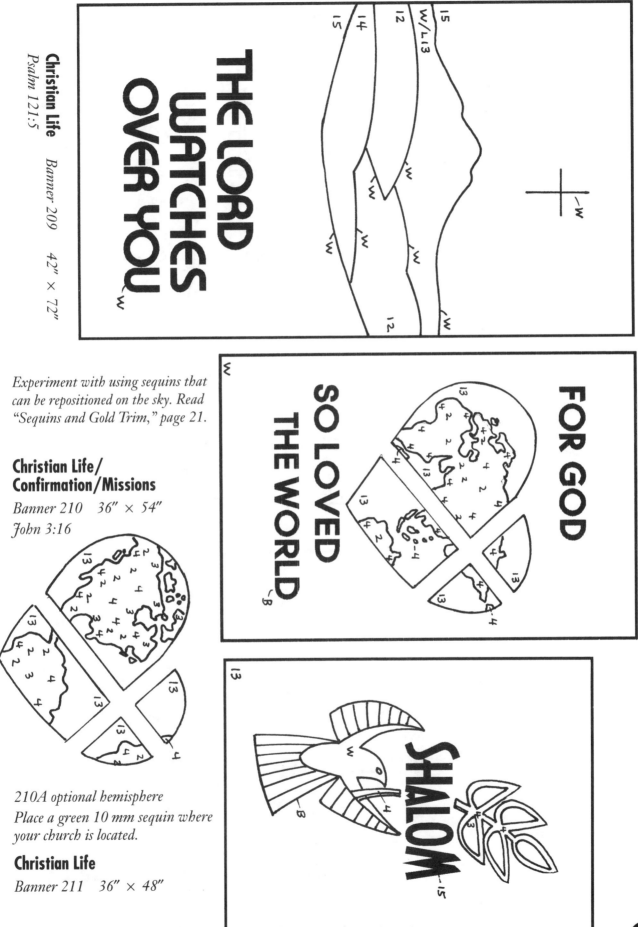

Christian Life
Psalm 121:5

THE LORD WATCHES OVER YOU

Banner 209   42" × 72"

Experiment with using sequins that can be repositioned on the sky. Read "Sequins and Gold Trim," page 21.

**Christian Life/
Confirmation/Missions**

Banner 210   36" × 54"
John 3:16

FOR GOD SO LOVED THE WORLD

210A optional hemisphere
Place a green 10 mm sequin where your church is located.

Christian Life

Banner 211   36" × 48"

SHALOM

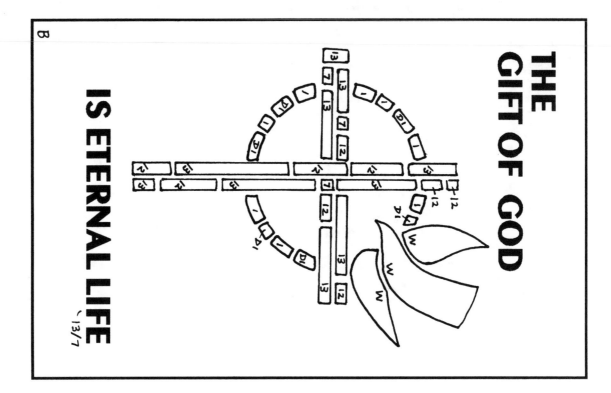

Christian Life/Funeral

Banner 212   45″ × 72″
Romans 6:23

Praise/Prayer

Banner 213   9″ × 48″

Christian Life

Banner 214
48″ × 63″
Reference to
Deuteronomy 10:12
Option: Use watercolor paints to color the globe like Banner 23A and use black (or white for greater contrast) felt lines for the hands. Read "Markers and Watercolor Paints," page 25.

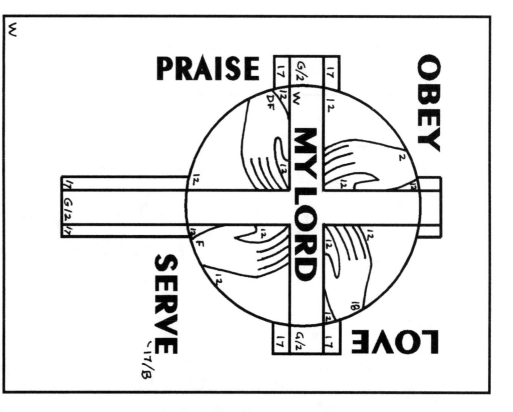

PRAISE GOD

GOD'S PROMISES ARE SURE

Christian Life   *Banner 215   36″ × 66″*
Read "Directions for Painting a Watercolor Rainbow," page 26, and "Sequins and Gold Trim," page 21.

Thanksgiving/Praise
Banner 215A

SERVE THE LORD WITH ALL YOUR HEART

Christian Life   *Banner 216   42″ × 69″*
1 Samuel 12:20

KYRIE ELEISON

Prayer/Praise   *Banner 217   9″ × 48″*
217–218 set of bans to be used individually or together
Prayer   *Banner 218*
Christian Life/Confirmation
Banner 219   15″ × 78″   *Option: Add any symbol design from this book or leave as is.*

LORD, BE IN MY LIFE

Christian Life
Banner 220
48" × 57"
Words are taken from the hymn "Amazing Grace."

Christian Life
Banner 221
9" × 72"

Christian Life
Banner 222
9" × 72"

Christian Life
Banner 223
45" × 72"

PART 3

Resources

COLORS OF THE CHURCH YEAR

Sundays and Major Festivals

The Time of Christmas

Advent Season—blue or purple

Christmas Season—white

Epiphany Season
The Epiphany of Our Lord—
white
The Baptism of Our Lord—
white
Second to Eighth Sunday after
the Epiphany—green
The Transfiguration of Our
Lord—white

The Time of Easter

Lenten Season

Ash Wednesday—black or purple

First to Fifth Sunday in Lent—
purple

Holy Week
Palm Sunday—scarlet or purple
Maundy Thursday—scarlet or
white
Good Friday—black

Easter Season
The Resurrection of Our Lord
Easter Eve—white
Easter Day—white or gold
Easter Evening—white or
gold
Second to Seventh Sunday of
Easter—white
The Ascension of Our Lord—
white
Pentecost—red

The Time of the Church

The Season after Pentecost

The Holy Trinity—white
Second to Twenty-seventh Sun-
day after Pentecost—green
Last Sunday of the Church
Year—green

Minor Festivals and Occasions

Eve of the Name of Jesus (New
Year's Eve)—white

The Circumcision of Our Lord
(New Year's Day)—white

Reformation Day—red

All Saints' Day—white

Dedication of a Church—red

Anniversary of a Congregation—
red

Mission Festival—white

Harvest Festival—color of the sea-
son

Day of Supplication and Prayer—
purple

Thanksgiving—white

SYMBOLS AND THEIR MEANINGS

Colors

blue—heaven, hope, truth, faith-
fulness
white—purity, holiness, inno-
cence, faith, light
green—growth, life, victory, hope
black—sin, evil, death
purple—repentance, royalty,
remorse
scarlet—royalty, loyalty
red—fire, presence of the Holy
Spirit, love

gold—eternity, marriage, God's
abundance

Christian Symbols

Alpha, Omega—eternity, Alpha:
beginning, first, Omega: end,
last
anchor—hope
bag of money—Judas' betrayal
with 30 pieces of silver
Bible—God's Word
butterfly with/without cross—res-
urrection, new life
castle turret—fortress, stronghold
chains—sin, evil, death
chalice—wine, Christ's blood,
Communion/Sacrament, for-
giveness
Chi Rho—first two Greek letters
in Christ
Christ's clothing—fulfillment of
the prophesy of casting lots for
His garments
cross of ashes—repentance
cross shaped as a star—Christ (Chi
Rho) the Light
cross—redemption, forgiveness,
salvation through Christ's
death
crosses (three)—two thieves on
crosses along with Jesus
crown of thorns—suffering, Christ
wounded for our sins
crown—royalty, kingdom, ruler,
king
crowns (three)—Wise Men
dove with an olive branch—peace
of God
dove—Holy Spirit
doves—wedding

Easter lily—resurrection, spring/new life

eleison—*have mercy*

empty cross—work of Christ's redemption is complete

fish/hook—mission, fishers of men

flame—Holy Spirit, Christ as the Light, faith, knowledge

globe—the world, mission, Great Commission

grain—bread/Christ's body, Communion/Sacrament, God's gifts, missions, harvest

grapes—wine/Christ's blood, Communion/Sacrament, God's gifts, forgiveness

halo—holy person

hand with blood drop—nail wounds from Christ's crucifixion

heart—love

holly and berries—the sharp points for Christ's crown of thorns, the red berries for Christ's blood shed on the cross

hosanna—*a Hebrew expression meaning "Save!" that became an exclamation of praise*

hyssop—plant used in Old Testament cleansing ceremonies, its stalk was used to hold a sponge of wine vinegar at the crucifixion

IHS—*the first three Greek letters of Jesus*

Immanuel—*God with us*

INRI—*Jesus of Nazareth King of the Jews*

ichthus—*fish, first Greek letters in the words "Jesus Christ Son (of) God Savior"*

Kyrie—*Lord*

lamp—knowledge

leaf/plant—growth, faith

lion with the lamb—eternal peace

mountains—power of God, looking up to God

musical note—celebration, sing, rejoice, praise

nails—nails that held Christ and the sign on the cross

NIKA—*victory, God conquers*

olive branch with leaves—peace

palm leaf—praise to the King, Palm Sunday

pattern of three—Trinity

pax—*peace*

praying hands—praise, repent, prayer, thanksgiving

rainbow—God's promises kept

rings—wedding, promise

rooster—Peter's denial of Christ

shalom—*peace*

sheep, lambs—people in the Lord's fold

shell/water—Baptism

shepherd's crook—Christ's care as the Good Shepherd

smoke—incense to God

spear—used at the crucifixion to pierce the side of Christ

Star of David—royal lineage of Christ, the King

star—sign of Jesus' birth

sun with rays—life, earth's blessings, radiance of God

tablets of stone—Ten Commandments

temple curtain—fulfilled prophesy of being torn in two at Christ's death

upright hand—God the Father, benediction, Great Commissioning

wafer—bread, Christ's body, Communion/Sacrament

washing of hands—Pilate

whip—used by soldiers to beat Christ

INDEX OF USAGE

The banner designs in this book are arranged according to season, theme, or occasion. Some banners may be appropriate for other occasions as well and have alternate wording provided along with the design. Banners are listed by number.

*Some banners may require omitting the banner's existing wording and putting new wording on the banner or a side ban.

ADVENT

1–4 (Set), 6, 7, 8, 9, 10, 11–14 (Set), 15

ANNIVERSARY (see Wedding)

ASCENSION

84

ASH WEDNESDAY

25, 44

BAPTISM

122, 151, 152, 153, 154, 155, 156, 157, 158, 159, 159A, 159B, 160

BLESSING

84, 84A, 102E

CHRIST

18A, 18B, 70, 102, 102F, 103, 103A, 104, 105, 106, 107, 108, 109, 110, 111, 112–116, 117, 118, 119, 120

CHRISTIAN LIFE

100, 101, 119, 123, 137, 137B, 139, 142, 171, 202, 203, 204, 205, 206, 206B, 207, 208, 209, 210, 210A, 211, 212, 213, 214, 215, 216, 219, 220, 221, 222, 223

CHRISTMAS

1, 3, 4, 11, 15, 16, 16A, 17, 18, 18A, 18B, 19, 19A, 20, 20A, 21, 22, 23, 125, 190A, 205B, 211

COMMUNION/MAUNDY THURSDAY

30, 46, 65, 72–73 Communion set

CONFIRMATION

18C Rev. 2:10*
49 Rev. 2:10*
84 Matt. 28:20
84B John 14:27
96A John 10:27
98 Ps. 23:1
99 Ps. 23:1
102D Matt. 28:20
102F John 14:6
103B Rev. 2:10
104, 105, 107
108 John 8:12
109 John 8:12
119 Phil. 1:21
120 John 15:5
137 Gal. 5:25
137A Eph. 2:8
147–147A Ps. 55:22
169A Matt. 24:35
176A 2 Cor. 5:20
183A with the design from 181, 182, or 183 Joshua 1:9
184 Rom. 1:16*
207 Rev. 2:10
207A Rev. 2:10
207B Rev. 2:10
210 John 3:16
210A John 3:16, 219

THE CROSS

13, 43, 44, 47, 62, 63, 64, 66, 67, 69, 94, 118, 185, 206

EASTER

3, 14, 18B, 32, 33, 50, 74, 75, 75A, 76, 77, 78, 79, 80, 81, 81A, 82, 102B, 102C

EPIPHANY

19, 19A, 20, 20A, 21, 22, 23, 24

FUNERAL (see Easter)

103A, 212

GENERAL

1, 18B, 23, 23A, 73, 135A, 177, 184A, 186, 217, 220, 223

GOD'S WORD

161, 162, 163, 164, 165, 166, 167, 168, 169, 169A, 170, 171, 172

GOOD FRIDAY

31, 34–43 people of Passion Week set, 47, 48–55 the Seven Last Words of Christ set, 56–62 artifacts set, 63, 64, 66, 67, 68, 69, 70, 71, 72, 73

GOOD SHEPHERD

22, 96, 97, 98, 99

GREAT COMMISSION

84, 102A, 182

HOLY SPIRIT (see Pentecost)

HYMNS

16, 19, 20, 21 "Away in a Manger"*
18 "From Heaven Above to Earth I Come"*; "Joy to the World"*; "Now Sing We, Now Rejoice"*; "Hark! the Herald Angels Sing"*

18A "All Hail the Power of Jesus' Name"
18B "Crown Him with Many Crowns"
22 "Oh, Come, All Ye Faithful"*
33 "Jesus Shall Reign"
76 "Jesus Lives! The Victory's Won"
85 "A Mighty Fortress Is Our God"
88–90 set, 91B, 92 set "Holy, Holy, Holy"
96 "I Am Jesus' Little Lamb"*
100 "Abide with Me"
102C "How Great Thou Art"
110 "Jesus, Savior, Pilot Me"*
121 Pentecost hymns that begin with "Come …"
134 "Holy Spirit, Light Divine"
172 "Thy Strong Word"
173, 190, 205A "Go Tell It on the Mountain"
175, 184, 186 "This Little Gospel Light of Mine"
177 "Hark, the Voice of Jesus Calling"
185 "Lift High the Cross"
194 "Blest Be the Tie That Binds"*
204 "Bless This House, O Lord, We Pray"
220 "Amazing Grace"

INSTALLATION (see Ordination)

LENT

13, 34–43 people of Passion Week set, 44–47 Lent—Events, 63, 64, 65, 66, 67, 68, 69, 70

MAUNDY THURSDAY
(see Communion)

MISSIONS

33, 88C, 102, 102A, 108, 173, 174, 175, 176, 177, 178, 179, 180, 181, 182, 183, 184, 185, 185A, 185B, 186, 187, 188, 189, 190, 205A, 210

ORDINATION

97, 98, 99, 191, 192

PALM SUNDAY

26, 27, 28, 29, 45

PASSION WEEK

29–33 cross-crown set of 5

34–43 people of Passion Week set

44–47 Lent—events

PENTECOST/HOLY SPIRIT

90, 95, 121, 122, 123, 124, 124A, 124B, 124C, 125–133 Fruit of the Spirit set, 134, 134A, 135, 136, 137, 138, 139

PRAISE

3, 9* "joy," "rejoice," "praise," or "glory," 127, 135, 140, 141, 148, 149, 150, 213, 215, 217

PRAYER

143, 143A, 144, 145, 146, 147, 147A, 213, 217, 218, 221, 222

REFORMATION

85

SPIRITUAL GIFTS

142

THANKSGIVING

140, 141, 142, 143A, 206A, 215A

TRANSFIGURATION

83

TRINITY

86, 87, 88–90 set, 91, 91A, 91B, 92 set of 3 bans, 93–95 set

WEDDING/ANNIVERSARY

125, 127, 129, 193, 194, 195, 196, 197, 198, 199, 200, 200A, 201, 202, 203, 204

WORD (see God's Word)